WORLD
HISTORY SERIES

The Spanish-
American War

Titles in the World History Series

The Age of Augustus
The Age of Exploration
The Age of Feudalism
The Age of Napoleon
America in the 1960s
The American Revolution
Ancient Chinese Dynasties
The Ancient Near East
Architecture
The Assyrian Empire
The Battle of the
	Little Bighorn
The Black Death
The Bombing of Pearl Harbor
Building the Transcontinental Railroad
The Byzantine Empire
Caesar's Conquest of Gaul
The California Gold Rush
The Chinese Cultural
	Revolution
The Civil Rights Movement
The Collapse of the
	Roman Republic
Colonial America
The Computer Revolution
The Conquest of Mexico
The Constitution and the Founding of
	America
The Creation of Israel
The Crimean War
The Crusades
The Cuban Missile Crisis
The Decline and Fall of the Roman
	Empire
The Early Middle Ages
Elizabethan England
The Enlightenment
Greek and Roman
	Mythology
Greek and Roman Science
Greek and Roman Sport
Greek and Roman Theater
The History of Medicine

The History of Rock & Roll
The History of Slavery
Hitler's Reich
The Inca Empire
The Industrial Revolution
The Inquisition
The Italian Renaissance
The Korean War
The Late Middle Ages
The Louisiana Purchase
The Making of the Atom Bomb
The Mexican-American War
The Mexican Revolution
The Mexican War of
	Independence
Modern Japan
The Mongol Empire
The Persian Empire
Pirates
Prohibition
The Punic Wars
The Reagan Years
The Reformation
The Renaissance
The Rise and Fall of the
	Soviet Union
The Rise of Christianity
The Roaring Twenties
The Roman Empire
Roosevelt and the
	New Deal
Russia of the Tsars
The Salem Witch Trials
The Space Race
The Stone Age
The Titanic
Traditional Africa
Twentieth Century Science
Victorian England
The Viking Conquest
The War of 1812
Westward Expansion
Women of Ancient Greece

WORLD
HISTORY SERIES

The Spanish-
American War

by
John F. Wukovits

Lucent Books, P.O. Box 289011, San Diego, CA 92198-9011

Library of Congress Cataloging-in-Publication Data

Wukovits, John F., 1944–
    The Spanish-American War / by John F. Wukovits.
      p. cm. — (World history series)
    Includes bibliographical references (p.) and index.
    Summary: Discusses the causes, events, and results of the Spanish-
    American War including the explosion of the USS *Maine*,
    American and Spanish military preparations, the Battles of Manila,
    Las Guasimas, El Caney, San Juan Hill, and Kettle Hill, Spain's
    surrender, and America's increased role in world affairs.
      ISBN 1-56006-682-2 (hardback : alk. paper)
    1. Spanish-American War, 1898—Juvenile literature.
    [1. Spanish-American War, 1898.] I. Title. II. Series.
      E715 .W85 2002
      973.8'9—dc21
                                                                00-013234

Contents

Foreword

Each year on the first day of school, nearly every history teacher faces the task of explaining why his or her students should study history. One logical answer to this question is that exploring what happened in our past explains how the things we often take for granted—our customs, ideas, and institutions—came to be. As statesman and historian Winston Churchill put it, "Every nation or group of nations has its own tale to tell. Knowledge of the trials and struggles is necessary to all who would comprehend the problems, perils, challenges, and opportunities which confront us today." Thus, a study of history puts modern ideas and institutions in perspective. For example, though the founders of the United States were talented and creative thinkers, they clearly did not invent the concept of democracy. Instead, they adapted some democratic ideas that had originated in ancient Greece and with which the Romans, the British, and others had experimented. An exploration of these cultures, then, reveals their very real connection to us through institutions that continue to shape our daily lives.

Another reason often given for studying history is the idea that lessons exist in the past from which contemporary societies can benefit and learn. This idea, although controversial, has always been an intriguing one for historians. Those who agree that society can benefit from the past often quote philosopher George Santayana's famous statement, "Those who cannot remember the past are condemned to repeat it." Historians who subscribe to Santayana's philosophy believe that, for example, studying the events that led up to the major world wars or other significant historical events would allow society to chart a different and more favorable course in the future.

Just as difficult as convincing students of the importance of studying history is the search for useful and interesting supplementary materials that present historical events in a context that can be easily understood. The volumes in Lucent Books' World History Series attempt to present a broad, balanced, and penetrating view of the march of history. Ancient Egypt's important wars and rulers, for example, are presented against the rich and colorful backdrop of Egyptian religious, social, and cultural developments. The series engages the reader by enhancing historical events with these cultural contexts. For example, in *Ancient Greece*, the text covers the role of women in that society. Slavery is discussed in *The Roman Empire*, as well as how slaves earned their freedom. The numerous and varied aspects of everyday life in these and other societies are explored in each volume of the series. Additionally, the series covers the major political, cultural, and philosophical ideas as the torch of civilization is passed from ancient Mesopotamia and Egypt, through Greece, Rome, Medieval Europe, and other world cultures, to the modern day.

The material in the series is formatted in a thorough, precise, and organized manner. Each volume offers the reader a comprehensive and clearly written overview of an important historical event or period. The topic under discussion is placed in a broad, historical context. For example, *The Italian Renaissance* begins with a discussion of the High Middle Ages and the loss of central control that allowed certain Italian cities to develop artistically. The book ends by looking forward to the Reformation and interpreting the societal changes that grew out of the Renaissance. Thus, students are not only involved in an historical era, but also enveloped by the events leading up to that era and the events following it.

One important and unique feature in the World History Series is the primary and secondary source quotations that richly supplement each volume. These quotes are useful in a number of ways. First, they allow students access to sources they would not normally be exposed to because of the difficulty and obscurity of the original source. The quotations range from interesting anecdotes to farsighted cultural perspectives and are drawn from historical witnesses both past and present. Second, the quotes demonstrate how and where historians themselves derive their information on the past as they strive to reach a consensus on historical events. Lastly, all of the quotes are footnoted, familiarizing students with the citation process and allowing them to verify quotes and/or look up the original source if the quote piques their interest.

Finally, the books in the World History Series provide a detailed launching point for further research. Each book contains a bibliography specifically geared toward student research. A second, annotated bibliography introduces students to all the sources the author consulted when compiling the book. A chronology of important dates gives students an overview, at a glance, of the topic covered. Where applicable, a glossary of terms is included.

In short, the series is designed not only to acquaint readers with the basics of history, but also to make them aware that their lives are a part of an ongoing human saga. Perhaps then they will come to the same realization as famed historian Arnold Toynbee. In his monumental work, *A Study of History*, he wrote about becoming aware of history flowing through him in a mighty current, and of his own life "welling like a wave in the flow of this vast tide."

Important Dates in the History of the Spanish-American War

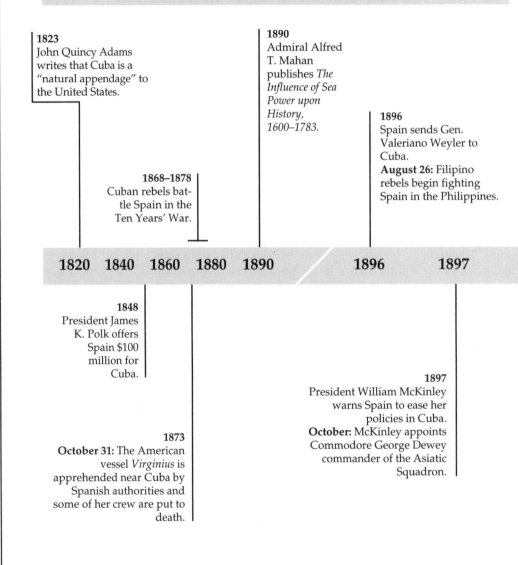

1823
John Quincy Adams writes that Cuba is a "natural appendage" to the United States.

1890
Admiral Alfred T. Mahan publishes *The Influence of Sea Power upon History, 1600–1783*.

1896
Spain sends Gen. Valeriano Weyler to Cuba.
August 26: Filipino rebels begin fighting Spain in the Philippines.

1868–1878
Cuban rebels battle Spain in the Ten Years' War.

1820 1840 1860 1880 1890 1896 1897

1848
President James K. Polk offers Spain $100 million for Cuba.

1897
President William McKinley warns Spain to ease her policies in Cuba.
October: McKinley appoints Commodore George Dewey commander of the Asiatic Squadron.

1873
October 31: The American vessel *Virginius* is apprehended near Cuba by Spanish authorities and some of her crew are put to death.

1898
February 9: American newspapers print the de Lôme letter.
February 15: The battleship USS *Maine* is sunk in Havana harbor.
March 8: McKinley asks Congress to approve a $50 million military expansion.
April 11: McKinley asks Congress for the authority to send military forces to Cuba.
April 21: McKinley declares a naval blockade of Cuba.
April 22: An American cruiser halts the Spanish merchant ship *Buenaventura*.
April 23: Spain officially declares war on the United States; McKinley issues a call for 125,000 National Guard volunteers.
April 24: Navy secretary John D. Long cables Dewey that war has begun and orders him to attack Spanish forces in the Philippines; Dewey departs Hong Kong for Manila Bay.
April 29: Admiral Pascual Cervera heads toward Cuba.
May 1: Dewey defeats the Spanish in the Battle of Manila Bay.
June 1: The U.S. Navy blockades Cervera in Santiago, Cuba.
June 3: Naval Constructor Richmond P. Hobson leads an attempt to block the channel leading into Santiago harbor.
June 6: U.S. Marines land at Guantanamo Bay, Cuba.
June 22: U.S. Army forces land in Cuba.
June 24: The Battle of Las Guasimas occurs.
June 30: Army units arrive in the Philippines to support Dewey's operations.
July 1: The Battles of El Caney, Kettle Hill, and San Juan Hill occur.

1976
A naval inquiry concludes that the *Maine* sank due to an internal explosion.

1898   1900   1976

July 3: The U.S. Navy defeats Admiral Cervera's force in the Battle of Santiago Bay.
July 10: American units begin the bombardment of Santiago.
July 13: Peace negotiations in Cuba commence.
July 17: Spanish forces in Cuba officially surrender to the United States.
July 25: U.S. Army units under Gen. Nelson A. Miles invade Puerto Rico.
August: The United States annexes the Hawaiian Islands.
August 12: McKinley signs the initial peace agreement with Spain.
August 13: Manila is seized by American forces, eliminating Spanish opposition in the Philippines.
December 10: The formal peace agreement ending the Spanish-American War is signed in Paris.

1902
May: The United States recognizes Cuban independence.
July 4: President Theodore Roosevelt declares the fighting in the Philippines over.

1901
March 23: Filipino rebel leader Emilio Aguinaldo is captured by U.S. soldiers.
September 28: A massacre of U.S. troops at Balangiga, Samar, leads to violent reprisals from American commanders.

1899
February 4: Fighting erupts between Filipino rebels and U.S. forces in the Philippines.

Little War, Big Effects

In an 1898 letter to politician, military officer, and future president Theodore Roosevelt, American secretary of state John Hay called the Spanish-American War the "Splendid Little War."[1] His remark summarized the prevailing view of the conflict at the time—that the strife between the United States and Spain was brief, glorious, and beneficial to the United States.

Hay's pointed comment contained much truth. Since the fighting between the combatants occurred in a four-month span, Hay was certainly correct in labeling it a brief event. Little doubt existed that its outcome boosted the United States to the top ranks of world powers while relegating Spain to the background. Whether it was a glorious war depended upon one's point of view—Spanish soldiers and officials, the American and Spanish families of those who died, and the soldiers who suffered serious wounds would find it more difficult to trumpet the glories of the war.

In any event the Spanish-American War, though one of the shortest in American history, produced results that reverberated long after the guns and cannons fell silent. Before the encounter, Spain enjoyed a position of respect among the world's nations while the United States—occupied with its own expansion throughout the North American continent and engaged in the catastrophic Civil War from 1861 to 1865—labored in Spain's shadow.

That changed in the 1890s. With the Civil War thirty years in the past and continental expansion all but completed, the United States looked outside her borders to increase her power and standing. American politicians wanted the United States to join the ranks of top world powers, and since other countries possessed colonies around the world, they believed that the fastest way to become equal to them was to control vast stretches of land in distant locales.

However, the United States needed to find uncolonized land to control. U.S. politicians had little desire to anger the strongest military powers, such as Great Britain, France, and Germany, whose battle-tested armies and navies posed formidable obstacles. It was in their best interest to seek a weaker foe, one whose fortunes were declining, and catapult to the top ranks of countries on the back of that nation's empire. Spain offered a promising opportunity, with its armies in disarray and with its colonial possession of Cuba posing a tempting target barely ninety miles off the Florida coast. However, Spain was reluctant to yield its position of authority to the upstart United States.

The resultant war between Spain and the United States began in April 1898 and officially ended in December 1898 with the signing of a formal peace agreement. Before hostilities ceased, fighting had occurred in and around islands in both the Atlantic and Pacific Oceans. Due to a combination of the modern U.S. Navy and the deplorable state of affairs in the crumbling Spanish military, the war ended much faster than observers had predicted. And it would produce effects more widespread than observers realized at the time.

THE BIRTH OF ONE EMPIRE, THE END OF ANOTHER

For starters, the Spanish empire that had existed since the days of Columbus in the late 1400s ceased to exist because of the war. Spain had enjoyed centuries of prosperity and power built mainly on the efforts of the brave and ruthless conquistadores, soldiers of fortune who crossed the Atlantic, established vast stretches of Spanish-controlled land in the New World, and robbed Native American peoples of their valuables. For years an endless succession of Spanish treasure ships weighed anchor in American and Caribbean ports and, bursting with gold and other valuables, headed toward Europe to fill the coffers of Spain.

However, through the years Spain faced a series of challenges from other nations, particularly France and England, and gradually its empire began to disintegrate. By the late 1800s, Spain's hold on its overseas possessions was greatly weakened, and the final vestiges of the empire collapsed with Spain's defeat by the United States in 1898.

At the same time, an American empire began. For much of the nineteenth century, politicians and businessmen in the United States had argued that the nation should own colonies around the world. With the successful conclusion of the war with Spain, the United States could now boast land in the Caribbean as well as control over the Philippines and other Pacific islands. The United States had joined the ranks of world powers.

The war had other effects too. It helped establish the reputation of a man who would eventually become one of the nation's most effective and popular presidents. Theodore Roosevelt had long labored in various state and national government posts, but it was his service in Cuba, where he and his Rough Riders gained fame, that catapulted him to national prominence. Within three years of the war's end, following the assassination of William McKinley, Roosevelt had risen to the presidency.

By far the most ominous aspect of the Spanish-American War was that it started the United States on a collision course with Japan. Since the United States now held interests in the Pacific, it was bound to compete for dominance with Japan, the other major power in the area, whose leaders also yearned to flex its military muscle. Japan, an island nation, needed to import raw materials and food from outside the country to fuel its factories and feed the people, and when Japan turned its hungry eyes to Pacific islands, the United States stood in the

Theodore Roosevelt and his volunteer regiment, the Rough Riders, rose to fame after their service in the Spanish-American War.

way. The resulting tension eventually led to a surprise Japanese attack on the American naval base at Pearl Harbor in 1941 that brought both nations into World War II as bitter foes.

The Spanish-American War thus produced far-reaching effects that stretched around the world. American proponents of the war touted its beneficial results—colonies, respect from other nations, a stronger navy, and popular heroes. As is so often true, though, good things come with a heavy price. In World War II, the United States had to pay the bill.

1 A Desire to Acquire Power and Wealth

The Spanish-American War had its roots in greed. Politicians in the United States wrapped it in a cloak of respectability by claiming they only desired to intervene in Cuban and Filipino affairs to help the native people gain better living conditions. But the real motivation was to accumulate property. Spain, which had created a potent empire by seizing other people's land in the New World, objected when the United States attempted to do the same to its possessions.

SPAIN ENTERS THE 1890S

As the final decade of the nineteenth century approached, Spain occupied a shaky position in world stature. Long accustomed to being viewed as a top power, the nation's leaders expected other European powers to give Spain the respect and fear which the country had always been accorded as a superpower. Unfortunately, Spain could no longer boast of the magnificent armies and splendid navies that had created its empire. A gradual decline caused by poor economic conditions, uninspiring leadership, and challenges by bombastic nations plagued the country.

By the 1890s, Spain retained only remnants of its once-majestic empire. After controlling much of Central and South America from the early 1500s to the early 1800s as well as large portions of land that now comprised Florida and the southwest section of the United States, Spanish possessions in the Americas had shrunk to only a few Caribbean islands, mainly Cuba and Puerto Rico. In the Pacific Ocean it governed Guam and the hundreds of islands that constitute the Philippines. The more its empire shrank, the harder Spain held on to what remained, for only in that manner could Spanish leaders believe that they still governed an empire.

But for Spain, the cost of administering land in the Americas and in the Pacific taxed Spanish resources. The nation no longer had a constant succession of treasure ships arriving to add to Spain's wealth. The Spanish navy fell into disrepair, and a nation that had once been feared by European rivals was now seen as only a minor irritant. As a result Spain rarely influenced world affairs as in the past, and its place atop the world rankings had been taken by Great Britain, France, and Germany. Spain now stood in the second tier of countries, ready to be replaced by a nation bearing resources, manpower, and an aggressive attitude.

THE SPANISH EMPIRE

Unlike 1898, Spain had once ruled the world. With the exploits of Spanish conquistadores such as Hernán Cortés in Mexico and Francisco Pizarro in Peru, Spain accumulated power and wealth the nation had never before possessed. In their 1998 book, The Americans, *Gerald A. Danzer, J. Jorge Klor de Alva, Louis E. Wilson, and Nancy Woloch describe the importance of Spain in the 1500s:*

"For Spain, the 1500s truly were golden. Spanish explorers blazed sea routes that spanned the globe, and they also plunged deeper into the Americas. For much of the 16th century, other European nations struggled to match Spain's power. During this time, the Spanish built a far-reaching overseas empire, which included New Spain (Mexico and part of what is now Guatemala), as well as lands in Central and South America and the Caribbean. While other European nations barely imagined American colonies of their own, the Spanish built immense cathedrals and a university in Mexico City."

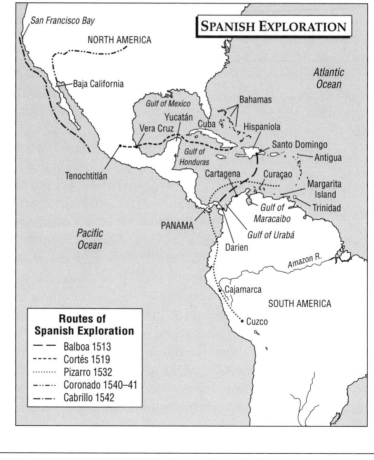

SPANISH EXPLORATION

San Francisco Bay

NORTH AMERICA

Atlantic Ocean

Baja California

Gulf of Mexico

Yucatán

Vera Cruz

Bahamas

Cuba

Hispaniola

Santo Domingo

Antigua

Gulf of Honduras

Cartagena

Curaçao

Margarita Island

Trinidad

Tenochtitlán

PANAMA

Gulf of Maracaibo

Gulf of Urabá

Darien

Pacific Ocean

Amazon R.

Cajamarca

SOUTH AMERICA

Cuzco

Routes of Spanish Exploration

— — Balboa 1513
----- Cortés 1519
········ Pizarro 1532
—··— Coronado 1540–41
—·—· Cabrillo 1542

THE UNITED STATES LOOKS BEYOND ITS BORDERS

While Spain was moving to the ranks of the lesser powers, politicians in the United States avidly wished to join the elite group of ruling nations. For most of the nineteenth century the nation's focus had remained within its own boundaries. Expansion into the West, economic policies, problems with Native Americans, and the Civil War had occupied the country's full attention.

That changed as the new century approached. Politicians and businessmen in the United States argued that the American people deserved to join the community of imperialist nations. For hundreds of years European countries had engaged in a race to accumulate a network of colonies in Africa, Asia, and the Pacific, each colony sending precious raw materials to the home country and each in turn providing a market for manufactured goods. This phenomenon of stronger nations controlling weaker nations, called imperialism, reached its high point in the nineteenth century, when the British Empire controlled lands around the globe.

Like Britain, owning colonies would help American industry. Business magnates needed raw materials from other lands to fuel the fantastic economic expansion which engulfed the nation following the destructive Civil War. Colonies could also benefit the United States by providing a new market for American-manufactured goods. U.S. citizens alone could not consume the vast amount of products pouring out of American factories and farms, but an overseas market controlled by the United States would eliminate the surplus and create a stream of money pouring into American banks.

Prominent Americans declared that the United States had a duty, a "manifest destiny," to reach beyond her borders. The nation had expanded from the Atlantic to the Pacific, but the imperialists saw no reason to stop there. Influential writer and promoter of American expansion, Adm. Alfred T. Mahan, stated that "Whether they will or no, Americans must now begin to look outward."[2] Others argued that the "more advanced" American people had a duty to spread religion and democracy to the less cultured portions of the globe and that the United States had a responsibility to civilize "backward" people. Lurking beneath these reasons, however, stood the real motivating drive—the desire to acquire wealth and power.

Mahan was a major proponent of this philosophy. In his influential 1890 book, *The Influence of Sea Power upon History, 1600–1783*, Mahan constructed a simple but powerful theory. Foreign markets were needed to purchase the surplus of goods produced by American factories. A large merchant marine had to be built to ship the products to overseas markets. To protect these ships and shipping lanes, the U.S. Navy had to be greatly expanded. Since American ships required coal to steam the oceans, coaling stations had to be established throughout the Pacific Ocean and other parts of the world, particularly in Hawaii and other islands.

Furthermore, with its growing interest in the Far East, the nation needed to be able to move its fleet quickly from ocean to ocean. This would depend on construction

SPREAD THE AMERICAN WAY OF LIFE

For much of the latter half of the nineteenth century, Americans debated the wisdom of becoming entangled in world affairs. As quoted in Page Smith's history of the times, The Rise of Industrial America, *Sen. Albert Beveridge of Indiana expressed the rise of the imperialist point of view when he spoke the following words in the 1890s:*

"We will establish trading posts throughout the world as distributing points for American products. We will cover the ocean with our merchant marine. We will build a navy to the measure of our greatness. Great colonies governing themselves, flying our flag and trading with us, will grow about our posts of trade. Our institutions will follow our flag on the wings of our commerce. And American laws will plant themselves on shores hitherto bloody and benighted, but by those agencies of God henceforth to be made beautiful and bright."

of a canal dug across Central America, in either Panama or Nicaragua, that would shorten the then-required trip around South America by thousands of miles. And in order to protect the canal, the United States would need naval bases throughout the Caribbean Sea.

Wherever the country turned, however, either to the Far East or the Caribbean, Spain stood in the way. The Pacific island of Guam offered a convenient coaling station, but Spain controlled it. The Philippine Islands contained natural resources, splendid harbors for the U.S. Navy, and a willing market for the nation's goods, but it too was under Spanish dominance. The same situation existed in the Caribbean. Military bases in both Cuba and Puerto Rico could shield a future Central American canal from foreign threats, but Spain controlled both countries.

While Spain's presence might have posed a more significant problem fifty years earlier, American expansionists now saw an opportunity to accumulate power at the expense of Spain. A determined campaign backed by a strong military could fashion a new American empire on the remains of the old Spanish empire.

Powerful American politician Henry Cabot Lodge expressed the American imperialist viewpoint when he wrote in *Forum* magazine,

From the Rio Grande to the Arctic Ocean there should be but one flag and one country. In the interests of our commerce we should build the canal, and for protection of that canal and for the sake of our commercial supremacy in the Pacific, we should control the Hawaiian Islands, and maintain our influence in Samoa. England has studded the West Indies with strong places which are a standing menace to our Atlantic seaboard. We should have among those islands at least one strong naval station, and when the canal is built, the island of Cuba will become a necessity.[3]

INTEREST IN SPANISH COLONIES

As is evident in Lodge's words, Americans possessed a keen interest in the island of Cuba, lying a mere ninety miles off Florida's shores. In 1823 then secretary of state John Quincy Adams wrote, "These islands [Cuba and Puerto Rico] are natural appendages to the North American continent"[4] and should one day form a part of the nation. The islands commanded the sea lanes into the Caribbean and the Gulf of Mexico, provided protection for a canal, and Havana, Cuba, offered one of the choicest deepwater harbors in the world.

At the same time, American expansionists hungrily gazed toward Spain's possessions in the Pacific. Guam, located between the Philippines and Hawaii, offered a convenient coaling station for American ships making the lengthy ocean voyage, while the Philippines added resources and harbors for a major American naval base. Supported by such a strong naval bastion, the United States could protect merchant ships headed for the lucrative Far Eastern markets and could also assert its interests elsewhere in the Pacific.

President James K. Polk offered Spain $100 million for Cuba in 1848. The Spanish government, desperately clinging to its last vestiges of empire, declined the offer and stated that it would prefer to have the island disappear beneath the waves rather than allow it to fall into another nation's grasp. Though the rejection produced few repercussions in the immediate aftermath, it established the two nations as antagonists and ignited the first sparks that later flared into war.

The *Virginius* Affair of 1873 provided a second spark, and also brought Spain and the United States closer to war. On October 31, 1873, the American vessel *Virginius* was steaming toward Cuba with ammunition, supplies, and one hundred American rebels to reinforce native insurgent groups attacking Spanish locations. Spanish authorities

Politician Henry Cabot Lodge pushed for American control of Cuba.

had long been eager to seize the ship, which had been involved in gunrunning for a decade and was owned by Americans who cared for little but profit. A Spanish warship spotted the *Virginius* as it neared the Cuban coast, overtook the ship, and brought the vessel and crew to Cuba.

The next day a court-martial sentenced the ship's crew to death. Despite public outcries in the United States for leniency, on November 4 a firing squad executed four American crew members. The Spanish placed their decapitated heads on spikes and posted them as a warning to rebels.

Americans were repulsed by the harsh treatment accorded their fellow countrymen, and their wrath rose to a higher pitch when Spanish authorities shot forty-nine more Americans over the next few days. The American government, hoping to avoid war, placed increasing pressure on Spain to end the affair. Weary from battling Cuban rebels and beset with economic problems at home, the Spanish government finally agreed to release the ship and remaining crew members, and to distribute eighty thousand dollars to the families of the victims.

WEYLER ENTERS THE PICTURE

Fortunately, rebel forces on the island handed the United States an opportunity to become an imperialist power. While the United States pursued different options aimed at acquiring Cuba, Cuban rebels battled the Spanish occupiers in order to free their homeland from foreign oppression. The Ten Years' War (1868–1878) accomplished lit-

José Martí led Cuban rebels in hit-and-run attacks against Spanish forces during a revolution in the 1890s.

tle but misery and bloodshed. A second revolution in the 1890s, led by Cuban poet and journalist José Martí, employed hit-and-run attacks against Spanish forces and destroyed sugar mills and plantations in Cuba, including those owned by American business interests. The rebels hoped that this would incite the United States to intervene in Cuba or apply pressure on Spain to grant independence to Cuba, and thus end the attacks on American holdings.

The fighting in Cuba aroused segments of the American people. Business interests and imperialists saw a chance to expand American control outside the continent,

A Solitary Execution

Of the many newspaper reporters who covered events before and during the Spanish-American War, journalist Richard Harding Davis was the most famous. He had built a solid reputation throughout his career, and thousands of people awaited his reportage in the New York Journal *and in* Harper's *magazine. In one of his most renowned pieces, which he called "The Death of Rodriguez," Davis recounted the execution of a Cuban rebel in the town of Santa Clara. The words are taken from G. J. A. O'Toole's book,* The Spanish War.

"He had a handsome, gentle face of the peasant type, a light, pointed beard, great wistful eyes, and a mass of curly black hair. He was shockingly young for such a sacrifice.

The officer of the firing squad hastily whipped up his sword, the men leveled their rifles, the sword rose, dropped, and the men fired. At the report the Cuban's head snapped back almost between his shoulders, but his body fell slowly, as though some one had pushed him gently forward from behind and he had stumbled. He sank on his side in the wet grass without a struggle or sound, and did not move again.

The whole world of Santa Clara seemed to stir and stretch itself and to wake to welcome the day just begun. But as I fell in at the rear of the procession and looked back, the young Cuban, who was no longer part of the world of Santa Clara, was asleep in the wet grass, with his motionless arms still tightly bound behind him, and the blood from his breast sinking into the soil he had tried to free."

Richard Harding Davis (right) reported the events of the Spanish-American War in the New York Journal.

while well-meaning individuals, such as the American Red Cross's Clara Barton, truly hoped to aid the downtrodden Cuban masses. They combined forces and urged President Grover Cleveland either to threaten military action or at least send diplomats to Spain to negotiate a settlement to the revolution.

Spain adopted steps of its own. To correct the unrest in Cuba, in 1896 Spain dispatched Gen. Valeriano Weyler, a no-nonsense military commander who intended to show the rebels that Spain, not Cubans, held the upper hand. He wasted little time implementing his moves, especially the controversial policy of removing entire Cuban populations from their cities and villages and herding them into concentration camps. By confining Cuban citizens to the camps in his so-called "reconcentration" policy, Weyler believed that the rebels would lack the base of support from which they had drawn so much strength in the past. No longer could they count on villagers to hide them or

Cuban rebels cook a pig at their camp during an insurrection against Spanish occupiers in 1898.

gather sorely needed food and supplies. The rebels would be forced out of the jungles, drawn into a fight, and eliminated.

Weyler also played on human emotions. He understood that many of the rebels would have family and friends among the people confined to the camps. Weyler would use the hostages to demoralize the rebels and force them to cease fighting.

Weyler's tactics, although effective, proved inhumane. The Cubans, coerced into the camps, huddled in inadequate huts with few toilets or finished roofs. Most individuals had to sleep outside or in hallways, and the food, what little there was, could not satisfy the demand. According to one Spanish estimate, over a two-year span, one-third of the Cuban rural population—almost four hundred thousand people—died in the camps.

CLOSER TO WAR

A growing number of Americans became outraged over Weyler's ironfisted rule. They objected partly for humanitarian reasons, but mainly because it gave them another reason to take action in Cuba. A February 23, 1896, article in the *New York Journal* called Weyler a "fiendish despot, a brute, the devastator of haciendas [homes], pitiless, cold, an exterminator of men. There is nothing to prevent his carnal, animal brain from running riot with itself in inventing tortures and infamies of bloody debauchery."[5]

Commander George A. Converse of the U.S. Navy visited Cuba during Weyler's tenure and reported to superiors that the "distress was no longer confined to the laboring country people, most of whom have already perished, but has now extended to the upper classes, who before the war were in moderately comfortable circumstances."[6] He added that when he and his crew members went ashore, starving men, women, and children begged for food.

Spain directed harsh words toward its American critics. One pamphlet labeled the Americans "these Yankee pigs who meddle in our affairs, humiliating us to the last degree," and exhorted loyal countrymen to remain steadfast. "Spaniards! The moment of action has arrived. Do not go to sleep! Let us teach these vile traitors that we have not yet lost our pride, and that we know how to protest with the energy befitting a nation worthy and strong, as our Spain is, and always will be!" The pamphlet ended, "Death to the Americans! Long live Spain! Long live Weyler!"[7]

Many people in Spain swore that they would die before allowing another power to strip the nation of its last traces of empire. When one official there threatened to sacrifice the entire treasury and the last blood of the last Spaniard to hold onto colonial lands, many Spanish heads nodded in agreement.

War between the two nations drew closer. Further events in the 1890s, heated to an intense pitch by inflammatory newspaper articles and headlines, set the stage for military action.

Chapter

2 "A Terrible Mass of Fire and Explosion"

The years 1895–1898 brought the United States and Spain into open conflict. Relations between the two countries—one desperately clinging to an empire, the other fervently hoping to construct an empire—soured as debate intensified about Spain's treatment of Cuban rebels. Sensationalistic newspaper accounts in the United States, depicting Spain as an evil overseer grinding the freedom-loving Cuban peasants under its heel, created a public demand for military action, and expansionist advocates in and out of Congress gained momentum in their campaign to possess colonies. Little would be required to nudge the nations toward war, and by the middle of February 1898 two events handed the United States all the justification the nation would need to actively intervene.

AMERICA DIVIDED

Ironically, while some politicians adopted a bellicose stance toward Spain, the two presidents of the 1890s at first worked for peace. They realized that war, instead of being an event to be excited about, offered only death and misery. Grover Cleveland thought that the belligerent attitude which swept the na-

tion was an example of "an epidemic of insanity in the country."[8]

His successor, William McKinley, who served from 1897 until his death by an assassin's bullet in 1901, had seen fighting and death in the Civil War. He planned to imitate Cleveland's effort. McKinley hoped to curb the lust for possessions that seemed

President William McKinley attempted to avoid war with Spain at the beginning of his presidency.

THEODORE ROOSEVELT

Theodore Roosevelt experienced a fascinating life both before and after the Spanish-American War. After graduating from Harvard, he served in the New York State Assembly for the Republican Party, wrote numerous books and articles, including a highly regarded naval history of the War of 1812, started a cattle ranch in the desolate Dakota Badlands, and reformed the New York City Police Department in his role as commissioner. Roosevelt's presidency (1901–1909) dominated his postwar life, which he supplemented with frequent hunting forays around the world. When the United States entered World War I in 1917, Roosevelt, nearing sixty years of age, asked for another military command, which the government wisely declined to grant.

Theodore Roosevelt poses with his kill after one of his frequent hunting trips.

to have gripped so many people in the nation, and he admonished associates that war should never be undertaken until every other step had been tried. McKinley mentioned to Cleveland as he took office, "Mr. President, if I can only go out of office at the end of my term with the knowledge that I have done what lay in my power to avert this terrible calamity with the success that has crowned your patience and persistence, I shall be the happiest man in the world."[9]

Unfortunately, the two presidents were unable to stop the growing momentum leading to war, and finally McKinley saw little alternative to military action. Each year the expansionists gained strength, led by politicians such as Theodore Roosevelt, then assistant secretary of the navy. The future president leaped at the opportunity to prove his mettle in battle and stated, "No national life is worth having if the nation is not willing, when the need shall arise, to stake everything on the supreme arbitrament of war, and to pour out its blood, its treasures, its tears like water rather than to submit to the loss of honor and renown."[10]

NEWSPAPER WAR HELPS CREATE REAL WAR

Roosevelt and other expansionists enjoyed potent allies in the New York newspaper industry. Two giants of the time, William Randolph Hearst's *New York Journal* and Joseph Pulitzer's *New York World*, engaged in a heated newspaper war for customers. Newspapers provided the main source of information for the American public in those days. Radio, television, and the Internet were far in the future, and if people wanted to learn what was going on in the world around them, they turned to one of the daily newspapers.

America's largest city, New York, boasted eight morning and seven evening daily newspapers, and an equal number of weekly publications for its population of 2.8 million. Competition for readers was intense. Teasing headlines in the *World* tried to outdo lurid ones in the *Journal*. Pulitzer hired reporters to unearth scandal in politics and shame in city government. Female reporter Nellie Bly posed as an insane person to gain admittance to a mental institution so she could research reported abuses there. Hearst believed that the public wanted to be shocked and entertained, and he thus ordered his editors and reporters to write in what was labeled a "gee whiz!" fashion. When events did not suit their interests, Hearst and Pulitzer created news stories in order to sell more papers.

The two publishing magnates saw a profitable opportunity in Cuba, where Spanish oppression of downtrodden peasants created perfect copy for their newspapers. Both dispatched their top reporters and artists to the island with orders to find examples of treachery by the Spanish, even if the facts had to be distorted. Some reporters, eager to please their bosses, grossly exaggerated accounts of Spanish actions and labeled General Weyler "the Butcher." With the flick of a reporter's pen, single gunshots heard in the distance became volleys of fire against unarmed Cubans; minor skirmishes turned into violent clashes. Unsubstantiated stories circulated that Spanish soldiers poisoned water wells and tossed Cuban children to the sharks. Torture and atrocities, whether verified or not, became the staples of daily reporting.

Hearst asked the famous artist Frederic Remington to draw sketches of the fighting in Cuba between the Spanish and the rebels. When Remington wondered what he should do if he found little fighting, Hearst replied, "You furnish the pictures, and I'll furnish the war."[11] Hearst was willing to include incendiary articles and drawings, even if it meant bloodshed, to gain additional subscribers to his newspaper.

While Hearst and Pulitzer tallied their profits, sentiment for military action against Spain was building throughout the country. In 1897, McKinley informed the Spanish government that unless it enacted measures to improve conditions in Cuba for the native population, including replacing General Weyler, he would have little choice but to take steps to ensure peace on the island. McKinley's minister to Spain, Stewart L.

Woodford, explained to Madrid officials that the United States could hardly stand by and watch another nation in the Western Hemisphere be systematically ravaged by a European power.

Spanish leaders knew that the U.S. stance contained a dose of hypocrisy, for the United States was more interested in grabbing land than in protecting peasants. However, Spain at this juncture was unwilling to irritate a rising world power and agreed to McKinley's demands in September. In addition to replacing Weyler with the more humane Capt. Gen. Ramon Blanco, Spain halted the reconcentration policy, handed Cubans more control in their own government, and granted amnesty to political prisoners.

For the moment, war fever in the United States subsided. But the embers remained, dimmed yet glowing. It would only require a spark to once again ignite it.

An editorial in the *Washington Post* typified the feelings that much of America felt on the eve of war:

> A new consciousness seems to have come upon us—the consciousness of strength—and with it a new appetite, the yearning to show our strength, ambition, interest, land hunger, pride, the mere joy of fighting, whatever it may be, we are animated by a new sensation. We are face to face with a strange destiny. The taste of Empire is in the mouth of the people even as the taste

A nineteenth-century cartoon depicts the rivalry between publishers Pulitzer and Hearst. Both were eager to profit from a war with Spain.

of blood in the jungle. It means an Imperial policy, the republic taking her place with the armed nations. [12]

THE DE LÔME LETTER

The first spark came from the hands of a respected diplomat. Enrique Dupuy de Lôme, the Spanish minister to the United States, wrote a letter to Jose Canalejas, an eminent Spanish politician and newspaper editor, in which he discussed the present crisis in Cuba. Most of the letter contained harmless information and opinions, but one section included de Lôme's harshly critical view of President McKinley. The diplomat wrote his friend that the American president was "weak and a bidder for the admiration of the crowd, besides being a would-be politician who tries to leave a door open behind himself while keeping on good terms with the jingoes [interventionists] of his party." [13]

Comments such as these were harmless in a confidential letter, but once made public they inflamed an already tense situation. Cuban rebels stole the letter from the Havana post office and, realizing its public relations value in the United States, offered it to both the *New York Journal* and *New York World*.

Their move produced the desired results. When William Randolph Hearst's *Journal* published the letter on February 9, outraged Americans demanded action ranging from de Lôme's resignation to outright war. Ironically, if one of McKinley's opponents in Congress had made similar remarks, they would have been seen as typical political maneuvers. But these comments had come from a foreign diplomat, and most Americans took offense to this attack on their president.

De Lôme, realizing that his rash action impeded chances of lasting peace between his nation and the United States, offered his resignation. Meanwhile McKinley urged caution in Washington, D.C. Fortunately, cooler heads prevailed in this instance. De Lôme's resignation and a Spanish apology defused the situation. Within six days, Americans who wanted war with Spain had their justification anyway. This time a ship, not a letter, provided the incident.

THE EXPLOSION ABOARD THE USS *MAINE*

With political and military turmoil gripping Cuba, the American consul general in Havana was worried about the safety of American citizens residing on the island. He urged President McKinley to dispatch a warship to Havana harbor as a sign of strength and as a warning to Spain that the United States intended to protect its citizens.

In an effort to join the ranks of world powers, the United States had embarked on a widespread expansion of the navy. Among the new ships was the USS *Maine*, a steel battleship crewed by 355 officers and men. Instead of sails, huge steam-driven engines powered the gleaming vessel through the seas. In place of wooden hulls, a more durable steel frame shielded the men from danger. Americans looked with pride toward the nation's new warships, especially the gigantic ones such as the *Maine*.

The USS Maine, *commanded by Capt. Charles D. Sigsbee, enters Havana harbor in 1898.*

On January 24, 1898, McKinley ordered the *Maine* to Cuba with instructions to drop anchor in Havana harbor in plain view of the Cubans and the Spanish. The following afternoon the ship, commanded by Capt. Charles D. Sigsbee, proudly steamed into Havana harbor, dropped anchor, and fired the traditional cannon salute to the Spanish authorities. Sigsbee had purposely waited until midday to enter, when he knew that thousands of Cubans and Spaniards would be working or shopping in the harbor district and would thus see the *Maine*'s arrival.

The ship floated peacefully in the harbor for three weeks. At 8:45 P.M. on February 15, most of the crewmen were relaxing in one of the ship's rooms belowdecks or had already turned in for a night's sleep. Stars filled the skies overhead while officers aboard the warship leisurely strolled about the *Maine*, checking the handful of men on duty.

Captain Sigsbee was enjoying the calm as well. Sitting in his cabin as the *Maine* rocked gently in the waters, he listened to the ship's bugler sound taps, the signal to the rest of the crew to extinguish lights. "I laid the pen down to listen to the notes of the bugle which were singularly beautiful in the oppressive stillness of the night,"[14] he later recalled. He then turned his attention to a long-overdue letter to his wife, and had just finished when a terrifying explosion rocked the ship.

Sigsbee hurried out of his room and down a darkened passageway to the bridge. The executive officer (second in command), Lt.

A deadly explosion blasts through the Maine *on February 15, 1898.*

Cmdr. Richard Wainwright, and some other officers joined Sigsbee, but few other officers or crew appeared. Most had either been killed instantly by the ferocious first explosion, scalded to death by steam escaping from cracked boilers, or were drowned when water gushed in through fractures in the ship's hull.

Lieutenant Robert Hood was sitting on the port [left] side of the ship with his feet resting on the railing when the explosion occurred. He sought shelter behind a metal ledge. When he looked to the water near the ship, he noticed wounded men and pieces of the *Maine* whirling in the foaming harbor. Three other members of the crew ran on deck from below to see what could be done about saving the ship, but fires ravaged the sinking vessel.

As more survivors appeared from below, Captain Sigsbee posted guards about the rails in case Spanish boarding parties attempted to seize the *Maine*. After receiving reports from officers and from observing conditions, Sigsbee realized that the ship was sinking. Fearing that the fires would ignite ammunition stored below, he ordered everyone off the doomed vessel. In minutes the *Maine* settled on the harbor's bottom, with only the topmost portions resting above the water.

Famed American nurse Clara Barton was working in Havana when she heard the explosion. She later recalled, "The house had grown still; the noises on the street were dying away, when suddenly the table shook from under our hands, the great glass door opening on to the veranda, facing the sea,

CLARA BARTON

The youngest of five children, Clarissa Harlowe Barton was born on Christmas Day, 1821, in North Oxford, Massachusetts. Barton did well in school and at age seventeen entered the teaching profession. Shortly before the Civil War erupted in 1861, Barton moved to Washington, D.C., to work for the U.S. Patent Office, the government division that grants inventors legal ownership of their creations. After war broke out, however, she resigned her post to work with the wounded. By 1864 her tireless efforts had earned Barton the position of superintendent of Union nurses.

In 1869, Barton traveled to Europe for much-needed rest. While there she learned of the Red Cross, an organization dedicated to improving the plight of men wounded in bat-

tle. She quickly returned home where she labored to start a similar institution in the United States. She eventually succeeded and in 1881 the American Red Cross opened with Barton as its first president. She served in this capacity until 1904, when she retired to Glen Echo, Maryland. Barton died on April 12, 1912, from complications due to a severe cold.

Renowned nurse Clara Barton founded the American Red Cross in 1881.

The tremendous force of the explosion on the Maine *turned the steel battleship into a twisted heap of metal.*

flew open; everything in the room was in motion or out of place."[15]

A passenger sitting on a deck chair on another ship in the harbor, Sigmund Rothschild, glanced toward the *Maine* to see its bow [front portion] rise two feet into the air, then settle to the bottom. "It couldn't have been more than a few seconds after that noise that there came in the center of the ship a terrible mass of fire and explosion, and everything went over our heads, a black mass. Then we heard the noise of falling material on the place where we had been."[16]

American newspaper correspondents George Bronson Rea and Sylvester Scovel were sitting in a Havana café when the explosion shattered windows and lit up the harbor as if it were midafternoon. Eager to learn what had happened, the two rushed to the waterfront and jumped into a boat. As they headed toward the blazing scene, Rea looked at the once-proud *Maine*.

> Great masses of twisted and bent iron plates and beams were thrown up in confusion amidships [middle of the ship]; the bow had disappeared; the foremast [front mast] and smoke stacks had fallen; and to add to the horror and danger, the mass of wreckage amidships was on fire, and at frequent intervals a loud report, followed by the whistling sound of fragments flying through the air, marked the explosion of a six-pound shell.[17]

Other ships in the harbor quickly moved to help the *Maine*, including the Spanish cruiser *Alfonso XII*, but there was little they could do for three-fourths of the crew. Although American sailors scrambled off the stricken ship with due haste, 260 of the 355 men either died in the blast or shortly after. Survivors clung to debris in the water or swam to approaching boats.

The wounded, some badly burned or suffering from gaping wounds, were taken to a Spanish hospital on shore, where Spanish physicians treated the men with tenderness and efficiency. Clara Barton rushed over to help and walked into a setting that reminded her of the horrors of previous wars in which she had served. The nurse later wrote that American sailors

> had been crushed by timbers, cut by iron, scorched by fire, and blown sometimes high in the air, sometimes driven down through the red hot furnace room and out into the water, senseless, to be picked up by some boat and gotten ashore. Their wounds were all over them—heads and faces terribly cut, internal wounds, arms, legs, feet and hands burned to the live flesh.[18]

One unfortunate sailor lay sightless in his bed, unable to see because the concussion from the explosion blew out both eyes.

Later that night Sigsbee wrote a dispatch to Washington explaining the situation. In light of the tragic events, his telegram was remarkably restrained and even-tempered. After mentioning the damage, Sigsbee requested assistance for the surviving crew. "No one has clothing other than that upon him. Public opinion should be suspended until further report. All officers believed to be saved. Many Spanish officers including representatives of General Blanco now with me to express sympathy."[19]

REACTION IN THE UNITED STATES

Regarding public opinion, Sigsbee asked the impossible, for many U.S. citizens instantly concluded that Spain had set off the explosion. William Randolph Hearst immediately filled his front pages with coverage of the event, which he believed meant war for the nation and increased profits for his paper. Before any facts had been determined, one *Journal* headline proclaimed that "THE WARSHIP *MAINE* WAS SPLIT IN TWO BY AN ENEMY'S SECRET INFERNAL MACHINE."[20] Hearst printed an

After the Maine*'s explosion, American newspapers, including* The World, *carried inflammatory headlines.*

announcement that his newspaper would pay a fifty-thousand-dollar reward for information that linked Spain to the disaster.

A war cry swept across the nation: "Remember the *Maine!* To hell with Spain!"[21] Outraged citizens across the land, further enraged by the inflammatory newspaper accounts, demanded speedy action to teach the Spaniards that they could not attack the United States without fear of reprisal.

Assistant Secretary of the Navy Theodore Roosevelt proclaimed that the *Maine* had been "sunk by an act of dirty treachery on the part of the Spaniards,"[22] and hoped that before the day ended McKinley would order the navy to Havana. The eager young politician, never one to flinch from a challenge, offered his own services in the war.

However, McKinley wanted to wait until hard facts arrived before making any decisions. He said,

> I don't propose to be swept off my feet by the catastrophe. My duty is plain. We must learn the truth and endeavor, if possible, to fix the responsibility. The country can afford to withhold its judgment and not strike an avenging blow until the truth is known. The Administration will go on preparing for war, but still hope to avert it.[23]

BOARD OF INQUIRY SEEKS TO LEARN THE TRUTH

What McKinley awaited were the results of an official board of inquiry set up to examine the cause of the explosion. In the after-

After the Maine *explosion, an American newspaper depicted Spain as a blood-thirsty ape.*

math of the disaster, reports filtered in to John D. Long, secretary of the navy, that seemed to clear Spain of any involvement. Long learned that not only the *Maine* but other warships in the U.S. fleet had experienced problems in their coal bunkers. It seemed that the coal had a dangerous tendency to smolder if left sitting for too long. Before the *Maine's* sinking, crews of two other ships had discovered smoke in their coal bunkers which required them to immediately shovel out the coal and smother the smoke. Nearby wood had been charred in the incidents, signaling that they had come perilously close to explosions themselves. More than one dozen bunker fires had occurred aboard U.S. ships in the previous three years.

The *Washington Star* interviewed many naval officers, and most believed that the explosion occurred inside the *Maine*'s coal bunkers. Making the possibility even more likely, according to these officers, one of the *Maine*'s coal bunkers was next to an ammunition storage room.

As a result, Long confided to his diary on February 16, only one day after the explosion in Havana, his own naval experts were divided as to what destroyed the *Maine*. Some believed that a spark in the ship's coal bunker was to blame; others contended that only a mine of enormous power could destroy such a mighty ship. "There is an intense difference of opinion as to the cause of the blowing up of the *Maine*. In this, as in everything else, the opinion of the individual is determined by his original bias."[24]

Diplomats on both sides realized that the conclusions drawn by the board of inquiry would be instrumental in determining future relations between Spain and the United States. Theodore Roosevelt told a relative that no politician, including President McKinley, could restrain the fever for war should the inquiry announce the *Maine* was sunk by an external explosion. Juan Du Bosc, a Spanish official in Washington, D.C., reported to superiors that if the American naval inquiry "declares that the catastrophe was due to an accident, I believe I can assure your excellency that the present danger will be over, but if, on the contrary, it alleges that it was the work of a criminal hand, then we shall have to face the gravest situation."[25]

The members of the official board of inquiry, who felt increasing pressure to fault

Spain from Theodore Roosevelt and other politicians who favored war, concluded on March 21 that the explosion which tore apart the *Maine* had come from outside the ship, most likely from a mine. This handed imperialists and their allies the justification they needed for military intervention, and simultaneously impeded McKinley's efforts to halt the march toward war.

Spanish authorities carried out their own examination of the incident and claimed, not surprisingly, that an internal explosion

Secretary of the Navy John D. Long privately expressed his uncertainty about Spain's responsibility for the Maine *explosion.*

A Decent Man, an Agonizing Choice

President William McKinley knew the horrors of war firsthand because of his service in the Civil War. While many Americans were too young to recall that clash's brutalities and carnage, and thus opted for war in 1898, McKinley approached conflict with Spain with great reluctance.

In his history *The War with Spain in 1898*, David Trask quotes William McKinley as saying, "I shall never get into a war until I am sure that God and man approve. I have been through one war; I have seen the dead piled up; and I do not want to see another." McKinley added, "I do not care for the property that will be destroyed, nor the money that will be expended, but the thought of human suffering that must enter many households overwhelms me."

had destroyed the American warship. As evidence, they cited the lack of dead fish floating near the Maine, which would have occurred with an external explosion. They also stated that an external explosion would have caused a huge water geyser to spout upward from near the ship. No observers reported seeing one. Spain also argued that it made no sense for them to incite a war with the United States, so why should they authorize an attack? This explanation matches their actions in the tragedy's aftermath when Spanish officials went out of their way to assist the United States.

A giant leap toward war had been taken with the results of the American inquiry. Though a handful of diplomats on both sides sought peaceful solutions, events had been set on a course leading to open confrontation.

3 "There Are Limits to Everything"

After the board of inquiry announced its decision about the *Maine* explosion, events quickly dragged the United States and Spain toward hostilities. Theodore Roosevelt and other expansionists did what they could to nudge the United States into declaring war, while the Spanish government unsuccessfully attempted to solicit the aid of other European powers to bring about a peaceful solution. Military preparation, and the lack of it, helped determine the outcome before a single shell had been fired.

THE APPROACH TO WAR

Events in the United States worked against Spain. On February 25, Secretary of the Navy John D. Long took a day off work and placed his young assistant secretary, Theodore Roosevelt, in charge. Roosevelt, who long had carried a reputation for independent action and assertiveness, quickly took advantage of the opportunity by dashing off a series of orders preparing the navy for war. He alerted squadron commanders around the world to be ready to sail in an instant's notice; he had guns shipped from the Navy Yard in Washington, D.C., to New York to be fitted onto merchant marine ships; and he sent the Asi-

atic Squadron, commanded by Commodore George Dewey, to Hong Kong to fill its coal bunkers. Roosevelt also informed Dewey that if war erupted, "your duty will be to see that the Spanish squadron does not leave the Asiatic coast and then [to take] offensive operations in the Philippines." [26]

American imperialist Theodore Roosevelt aggressively pursued war with Spain.

President McKinley signs a resolution demanding that Spain grant independence to Cuba.

Roosevelt knew he might come under criticism for his actions, but he believed he acted in the best interests of the nation. He confided to his close friend, army surgeon Leonard Wood, that "I may not be supported, but I have done what I know to be right; some day they will understand."[27]

When Long returned to work the following day, he muttered to subordinates that "I find that Roosevelt, in his precipitate way, has come very near causing more of an explosion than happened to the *Maine*. The very devil seemed to possess him."[28] However, when Long reviewed Roosevelt's orders, he let them remain in force. Most were relatively harmless and did indeed help prepare the navy for conflict. The boldest step, the message to Dewey, simply reflected what most naval strategists believed should be done if war with Spain loomed.

Recognizing that public opinion and top leaders within his own party favored military action, McKinley took a more aggressive stance toward Spain. He alerted the Spanish government that if it wished to remain on stable relations with the United States, conditions for the Cuban people must improve. On March 8 he asked Congress to approve a $50 million military expansion, including the construction of three new battleships, sixteen destroyers, and fourteen torpedo boats. Later in the month he issued an ultimatum to Spain that it must cease the fighting in Cuba and grant Cuba its independence. However, the Spanish government stalled in the hopes that other European nations would try to negotiate a peaceful solution to the crisis.

Many Spanish citizens, especially those from the wealthier classes and members of the Spanish army, accused the United States of meddling in Spanish affairs. They believed that the only factor keeping the Cuban rebellion alive was the continued support from the United States, which they compared to Spain's attempting to force the United States to grant better conditions toward Native Americans. The Spanish government joined in the criticism and pointedly mentioned that the United States would never permit such interference into what it deemed an internal matter.

When the American Congress overwhelmingly approved McKinley's March 8 request and passed the Fifty-Million Dollar Bill on March 9, Spain reacted in disbelief. The near-unanimous congressional vote seemed to indicate that the United States was unified in its stance against the Spanish. Spain's military leaders were shocked that the U.S. Congress could allocate such a hefty sum of money without having to borrow the funds. Caught in an economic slump, Spanish officers could expect minor increases at best. The United States, on the other hand, appeared to be basking in money.

The Spanish government stood in a delicate situation. If it refused McKinley's ultimatum to grant Cuban independence, the nation faced war with the stronger United States. If the government agreed to the demand, it risked unrest, even possible rebellion, among angered citizens at home.

Spain Declares War

McKinley and other American leaders failed to appreciate the importance Spain placed on maintaining its honor. Spain had fought rebel forces in Cuba for much of the last thirty years. To simply yield control of the island after all the sacrifice, blood, and money would have been an insult to the soldiers, their families, and the proud heritage dating to the days of the conquistadores. Spain, a largely Catholic country, had long believed that its colonial possessions in America had been handed over by God as a reward for ousting the non-Christian Muslim armies from Europe in the thirteenth century.

Spain hoped that other European powers such as Germany, France, and Great Britain would intervene on its behalf. Should these nations, many also ruled by monarchs, act in concert, the great powers might force the United States to back down.

The Spanish queen, María Cristina, received momentary encouragement from the German ruler, Wilhelm II. He had mentioned in late 1897 that "It is high time that we other monarchs agree jointly to offer our help to the Queen,"[29] but he eventually backed down from the assertion. His nation and the other European powers were occupied with their own problems and, besides, none of them wanted to antagonize the United States.

The Spanish government's hope of acquiring help from fellow European countries was extinguished in the middle of March 1898 after Queen María Cristina wrote an impassioned letter seeking aid from her relative, England's Queen Victoria. The British government replied that while it sympathized with the Spanish, it could do nothing because of American strength in the hemisphere.

When other nations refused to become involved in the dispute, in early April,

Spain reluctantly agreed to negotiate with the United States. Queen María Cristina indicated, however, that her patience had been stretched to the breaking point. "The Americans intend to provoke us and bring about a war, and this I would avoid at all costs," she said. "But there are limits to everything, and I cannot let my country be humbled by America."[30]

Talks yielded few results. On April 11, McKinley asked Congress for the authority to intervene in Cuba to protect lives and property and to guarantee independence for the island. Nine days later Congress passed a resolution calling for Cuban independence, Spain's immediate withdrawal from the island, and the use of military action by the president if necessary. Congress also stated in the Teller Amendment, an amendment to the resolution, that the United States had no desire to absorb Cuba and that, if military action commenced, the forces would be pulled out as soon as order had been restored. Although the resolution was not a formal declaration of war, Spain felt it amounted to the same thing.

After receiving little support from other European countries, Spain's Queen María Cristina reluctantly agreed to negotiate peace with the United States.

Spain had little choice. Faced with the options of war on a distant island against a vastly stronger foe or rebellion at home, the Spanish government opted for violence overseas. David Trask, a prominent historian of the war, wrote of Spain, "In the end they accepted war, even though defeat all but seemed certain, because they believed that Spain could be preserved from revolution at home only by waging an honorable war abroad, no matter how disastrous the military outcome."[31]

On April 23, Spain rejected the demands set in the congressional resolution and declared war on the United States. The military conflict that William Randolph Hearst, Teddy Roosevelt, and most of the nation favored was about to happen.

AMERICAN ARMY PREPARATIONS

The American military quickly implemented its plan to battle Spain. Instead of crossing the Atlantic Ocean and taking the war directly to the Spanish homeland, army planners intended to send thirty thousand troops to attack Spain's Caribbean possession before Spanish reinforcements arrived. A military crossing of the Atlantic and an invasion of Spain itself would require immense forces and funds that could be put to better use elsewhere. In addition, army planners understood that the Spanish would fight with far greater determination should their own homeland be directly threatened. Army strategists believed that a more effective move would be to hit Spain's colonies, which could not be as easily defended and would not be fought for with as much vigor as Spain itself. Since Cuba stood

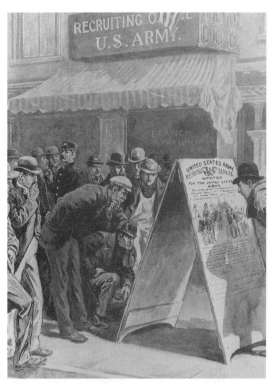

More than 1 million men volunteered to join the U.S. Army during the Spanish-American War.

ninety miles off the American shoreline, while the Philippines lay thousands of miles in the distant Far East, army planners centered the main thrust against Cuba.

On April 23, McKinley issued the call for 125,000 National Guard volunteers to supplement the Regular Army (each state organized its own National Guard units to be used as reinforcements for the army if the need arose). McKinley added a second call for another 75,000 soldiers in May. While this large number of soldiers reassured Americans, the much smaller Regular Army, which had to train these new troops, was overwhelmed. The army lacked sufficient supplies and training facilities for such a quick expansion, and the officers needed

So many men volunteered that the army was able to be selective and choose those most fit for service.

time to transform all these civilians into effective fighting men.

The training situation deteriorated under the increased demands. Hastily constructed camps in Florida were short of equipment and food. Men lived in unsanitary conditions, and adequate clothing failed to arrive. Soldiers wore winter uniforms and practiced with outdated rifles while trainloads of matériel lay abandoned on nearby sidetracks because no one had organized an effective way to move the supplies to camp. Hungry soldiers, forced to eat army canned beef that had been sitting in warehouses since the Civil War, scornfully called the rot-ted meat embalmed beef. So many boxcars accumulated near the main training base at Tampa, Florida, that movement on the rails halted for fifty miles around the city.

Despite these problems, the nation rallied to the cause. When additional appeals went out for soldiers, more than one million young men swamped recruiting stations all over the United States, enabling the army to be highly selective. Men had to be between the ages of eighteen and thirty-five, be of good character, free of disease, able to speak English, and be a citizen of the United States. In the end, the army accepted only 23 percent of the men who asked to join.

American Soldiers

Many men entered as a unit. The infamous outlaw Frank James (Jesse's brother) volunteered to lead a company of cowboys, and stories circulated that six hundred Sioux warriors hoped to travel to Cuba, battle the Spanish, and collect scalps. The *Journal* even printed an absurd statement that one decent-sized group of American athletes, who could not be stopped by Spanish bullets, would frighten the Spanish into surrendering simply by showing up.

Most notable was the unit organized by the aggressive Theodore Roosevelt—the First Volunteer Cavalry, called the Rough Riders. Comprised mainly of Roosevelt's New York friends and his acquaintances from time spent in the West as a sheriff and cowboy, the Rough Riders included New

Female Correspondent

Newspaper correspondents poured into Tampa, Florida, to cover the assembling American invasion force and the attack on Cuba. Among their numbers were two extraordinary females, Anna Northend Benjamin from *Leslie's* magazine and Kathleen Blake Watkins of the *Toronto (Canada) Mail and Express*.

In his book *The Correspondents' War*, Charles H. Brown relates that the women battled many obstacles simply to collect facts for their stories. "They received a cold shoulder, for the most part, from their male confreres and of course had no standing at all with the War Department, which was even reluctant to accept women as nurses."

However, through persistence and hard work Benjamin unearthed information on the scarcity of food for soldiers gathering in Tampa and on the Rough Riders' habit of helping themselves to local pigs and chickens when hungry. She wrote, "In truth, they did so make free with everything that they came across on the way down [to Tampa] that their fame spread on before them, and when they reached Tampa Colonel [Leonard] Wood was greeted with a petition from Tampa citizens requesting him to keep the Terros [the Rough Riders] within camp bounds."

Watkins also proved to be equal, if not superior, to the male correspondents by carefully developing sources of information in Florida and by talking to every available officer. Charles E. Hands, male correspondent for the *London Daily Mail*, wrote that "In a little while she was introducing *us* to generals and colonels. Before the evening was out she gave us the full details of an expedition to send arms and stores to the insurgents [in Cuba]—news which we had unsuccessfully been trying to get out." Hands added that the men so admired Watkins's professionalism that another correspondent exclaimed, "By gosh, she's hot stuff. She's one of the boys."

York City policemen, college football quarterbacks, cowboys and Indians, sheriffs, gamblers, and clergymen. Wealthy eastern businessmen mingled with westerners bearing names like Rattlesnake Pete, and Roosevelt warned his rich associates that they must be prepared to suffer the same inconveniences and dangers as everyone else. Officials offered Roosevelt command of the regiment, but he declined in favor of his friend, Col. Leonard Wood. Roosevelt acted as second in command.

In a letter to a friend, Roosevelt described the Rough Riders

> as typical an American regiment as ever marched or fought, including a score of Indians, and about as many of Mexican origin [heritage] from New Mexico; then there are some fifty Easterners—almost all graduates of Harvard, Yale, Princeton, etc.,—and almost as many Southerners; the rest are men of the plains and the Rocky Mountains. Three fourths of our men have at one time or another been cowboys or else are small stockmen; certainly two thirds have fathers who fought on one side or the other in the Civil War.[32]

U.S. soldiers behaved more like college students attending the season's most crucial football game than they did like men about to engage in bloodshed and death.

Theodore Roosevelt (center) stands with the Rough Riders, a regiment of former cowboys, Ivy League graduates, and Native Americans.

Free Soldiers Fighting for Freedom?

Many African Americans rushed to join the military. They entered having few misgivings about the irony of the situation in which African Americans fought to help free another people while they yet had basic freedoms denied them in the United States. As quoted by Page Smith in The Rise of Industrial America, *George Prioleau, the African American chaplain of the Ninth Cavalry, a black unit, wrote the following to a local newspaper:*

Though denied basic freedoms in the United States, scores of African Americans volunteered to serve during the Spanish-American War.

"You talk about freedom, liberty, etc. Why sir, the Negro of this country is a freeman and yet a slave. Talk about fighting and freeing poor Cuba of Spain's brutality; of Cuba's murdered thousands, and starving reconcentradoes [camps]. Is America any better than Spain? Has she not subjects in her very midst who are murdered daily without a trial of judge or jury? Has she not subjects in her own borders whose children are half-fed and half-clothed, because their father's skin is black? Yet the Negro is loyal to his country's flag. He sings 'My Country 'Tis of Thee, Sweet Land of Liberty,' and though the word 'liberty' chokes him, he swallows it and finishes the stanza 'of Thee I sing.' "

All were eager to enter the fighting without delay. Roosevelt and his men typified the emotion by raucously singing together, "Rough, rough, we're the stuff. We want to fight, and can't get enough. Whoo-pee!"[33] Famed Old West buffalo hunter and law officer Buffalo Bill Cody bragged that thirty thousand Indian fighters could defeat Spain in two months.

Secretary Long considered his young subordinate's desire to charge into battle a foolish death wish that could terminate a

The New York Journal's *April 22, 1898, headline boldly announces President McKinley's order to blockade Cuba.*

ficers to high posts, including Gen. Fitzhugh Lee, the nephew of Confederate commander Robert E. Lee, and Gen. Joseph "Fighting Joe" Wheeler.

AMERICAN NAVAL PREPARATIONS

Secretary Long put into motion a three-step plan for the U.S. Navy. He first implemented President McKinley's April 21 order to blockade Cuba in order to prevent Spanish reinforcements from arriving and to isolate Spanish forces already on the island. The navy was to stand guard off of every major Cuban port on the north coast, plus patrol off the important southern port at Cienfuegos, which had railway lines connecting it to Havana. On April 22 the North Atlantic Squadron, a collection of armored cruisers and gunboats commanded by Rear Adm. William T. Sampson, left American waters, steamed the brief ninety miles to Cuba, and took station off the island with orders to intercept any vessels attempting to enter Cuban ports and to attack ships trying to leave Cuba.

Long positioned other portions of the navy off the U.S. East Coast to defend American coastal cities from bombardment from any Spanish ships that might burst through the blockade. Even an attack by a solitary Spanish warship could throw a major urban area into panic, so American ships plied the waters between Maine and Florida looking for intruders.

A third fleet, as a result of Roosevelt's earlier orders, had already begun planning for offensive action. In Far East waters, the ships

promising political career. On the other hand, Long admitted to an associate, "And, yet, how absurd all this will sound if, by some turn of fortune, he should accomplish some great thing."[34]

Soldiers looked to the future with optimism. They assumed that Spain, a former first-rate world power with third-rate capabilities, would pose few problems. On the American side, for the first time since the devastating Civil War split the country in half in 1861, all sections of the United States—North and South and West—joined hands in a common military endeavor. To signal that the bitter divisions of the Civil War now belonged to the past, McKinley purposely appointed former Confederate of-

of Commodore Dewey's Asiatic Squadron completed preparations for battle and headed for the Philippines. Their intent was to destroy the Spanish fleet in Manila harbor and seize control of the islands for the United States before Spain could shift other forces there from Europe or the Pacific. While his naval counterparts in the Atlantic steamed off Cuba or shielded American cities, Dewey enjoyed the assignment of entering into battle with the enemy and grabbing land for the United States.

SPANISH MILITARY PREPARATIONS

As the United States readied its navy and assembled an army, Spain adopted war measures of its own. Although Spain had stationed 150,000 troops in Cuba, 8,000 in Puerto Rico, 20,000 in the Philippines, and another 150,000 at home, most of the soldiers were ineffective. Units in Cuba and the Philippines had been involved in tiring conflicts with rebel forces, and their numbers had been decimated by battle losses, tropical diseases, and troops leaving the military due to lengthy separations from their families. Potential reinforcements in Spain could do nothing to aid their Cuban counterparts unless the Spanish navy first gained control of the seas from the United States, allowing it to ferry troops where needed.

That was never the case, as the Spanish navy had fallen into an abysmal state of disrepair. Ships manned by ill-trained crews and rigged with ineffective guns begged for overhauls, but in the tight economic times the Spanish government lacked the money to improve current units or add new ones.

Admiral Pascual de Cervera, commander of Spanish naval forces, realized the quandary he faced. His superiors expected him to take offensive action against the stronger American fleet, yet he lacked sufficient resources. If he steamed across the Atlantic to enter battle with the United States, no base existed where he could repair damaged ships. Meanwhile the United States possessed repair facilities less than one hundred miles away. In effect, any damaged ship would be as good as sunk.

At the outbreak of war, Cervera asked the Spanish minister of the marine, Segismundo y Merelo Bermejo, what the navy's objective was. Should he remain in Spanish waters to defend the homeland from an

Admiral Pascual de Cervera commanded the unprepared Spanish naval forces.

American naval attack, should he head to Cuba to engage the enemy, or should he steam off the American coast and bombard American cities?

Instead of concentrating all of Cervera's forces into one potent fleet, Bermejo split the ships into two units. He ordered one portion to remain off the coast of Spain and sent Cervera with the remainder to assist the forces in Cuba.

Cervera considered Bermejo's order a fantasy that would only result in the destruction of his ships and men. He knew his poorly equipped and undermanned ships posed little threat to the mightier U.S. Navy, and any order that sent him into battle seemed a foolish waste of resources. He wrote Bermejo that,

> I ask myself if it is right for me to keep silent, make myself an accomplice in adventures which will surely cause the total ruin of Spain. And for what purpose? To defend an island which was ours, but belongs to us no more, because even if we did not lose it by right in the war we have lost it in fact, and with it all our wealth and an enormous number of young men, victims of the climate [disease] and the bullets, in the defense of what is now no more than a romantic idea.[35]

When he failed to convince Bermejo to keep the entire fleet in Spanish waters, Cervera left Spain and steamed to the Cape Verde Islands off Africa's west coast. He commanded what seemed to be a formidable force of four cruisers, three destroyers, and three torpedo boats, but its outward appearance masked an array of troubles. Two of the torpedo boats had to be towed by other ships because of engine failure, and the large ten-inch guns had not even been installed on one cruiser. The other cruiser's keel was so thickly encrusted with barnacles from constant steaming that it could proceed at barely half its normal speed. Any U.S. battleship, each of which had superior speed and firepower, could single-handedly defeat Cervera's entire squadron.

Cervera, an experienced naval officer, realized that he commanded a fleet doomed to defeat. He wrote to an associate that,

> We are reduced, absolutely penniless, and they [the Americans] are very rich. My purpose is not to accuse, but to explain why we may and must expect a disaster. I am sure that we will all do our duty, for the spirit of the navy is excellent; but I pray God that all the troubles may be arranged without coming to a conflict, which, in any way, I believe would be disastrous to us.[36]

While a pessimistic Cervera headed across the Atlantic, Spanish officials in the Philippines readied their military for action. They planned to defend the islands' major city, Manila, by developing a string of forts around the city's northern, eastern, and southern land approaches. From these locations they would repel any American land assault. Bermejo ordered the Spanish navy currently in the Philippines to assemble inside Manila harbor, shield the city on its west flank, and defeat Dewey when he appeared.

Like the orders given to Cervera, these commands grossly ignored realities in the Philippines. In one day Commodore Dewey churned into Manila harbor, smashed the Spanish navy, and grabbed America's first major colonial possession.

4 A Lopsided Victory

Americans expected quick victories in Cuba. Surprisingly, they first came not on or near the island ninety miles off Florida's shores, but thousands of miles across the Pacific. Led by the meticulous planner, Commodore George Dewey, the U.S. Asiatic Squadron steamed out of Hong Kong only hours after the war's start, headed to the Philippine Islands, and defeated the Spanish fleet. The action eventually handed control of the Philippines to the United States and thrust America into the ranks of colonial superpowers.

GEORGE DEWEY

George Dewey, naval commodore of the U.S. Asiatic Squadron, graduated from the Naval Academy at Annapolis, Maryland, in June 1858. He first saw action at New Orleans during the Civil War, when he served under the legendary Capt. David Farragut. During that battle, Farragut had been warned by fellow officers that he could not attempt to take New Orleans by attacking up the Mississippi River because two hastily constructed Confederate forts blocked the way. Instead of listening to the warning, Farragut led the fleet directly to

the two forts, which were nowhere nearly as formidable as the reports indicated, and thus captured New Orleans.

This bold decision impressed the young Dewey, who took its lesson to heart. Farragut insisted on thorough preparation and involvement by senior officers in any detail, no matter how small. His personal bravery—the veteran captain loved to stand on

George Dewey commanded the U.S. Asiatic Squadron and defeated the Spanish fleet in the Philippines.

the ship's rigging [ropes] and bark out orders to other officers in the heat of battle—also enthralled Dewey. "Farragut always went ahead," wrote Dewey later. "Instead of worrying about the strength of the enemy, he made the enemy worry about his own strength."[37] Dewey learned that reports of enemy concentrations were frequently inflated and based on rumor rather than fact. He remembered this thirty-six years later in Manila.

Dewey settled into a productive if unexciting career after the Civil War. Since no conflicts beckoned, the future for a naval officer did not look bright, and he spent most of his time conducting geological surveys or shuffling paper at desks. By 1896 he had almost concluded that, without a war in which to nobly serve and gain notice, he had gone as far as he could in the military. He confided to a friend, "I don't want war, but without it there is little opportunity for a naval man to distinguish himself. There will be no war before I retire from the Navy, and I'll simply join the great majority of naval men [who retired without notice], and be known to history only by consulting the records of the Navy Department."[38]

Dewey had gained influential friends over the course of time, however. One, Theodore Roosevelt, remembered Dewey when the post of Asiatic Squadron commander opened. Realizing that war with Spain loomed as a clear possibility and that it would transform the resource-laden Philippines into a rich prize for anyone capable of seizing it, Roosevelt promoted Dewey for the job. He wanted an aggressive commander who could take action even though he might be out of contact with Washington, D.C., thousands of miles away. Roosevelt indicated that Dewey "was a man who could be relied upon to prepare in advance and to act fearlessly and on his own responsibility when the emergency arose."[39]

In October 1897, President William McKinley acted on Roosevelt's recommendation. He ordered Secretary of the Navy John D. Long to appoint Dewey commander of the Asiatic Squadron, a group of ships protecting American merchantmen steaming in the Far East.

DEWEY READIES HIS FLEET

Dewey's squadron, waiting for further orders in Hong Kong, consisted of six naval ships carrying 1,456 officers and men—the cruisers *Olympia* (Dewey's flagship), *Baltimore*, *Boston*, and *Raleigh*, and the gunboats *Concord* and *Petrel*—plus the lightly armed revenue service cutter *McCulloch*. In addition, Dewey cleverly purchased the collier *Nanshan*, a ship for transporting coal, and the steamer *Zafiro*, and then registered them as unarmed American merchant vessels. This enabled the ships to enter neutral ports during wartime and purchase coal and other supplies, which international law at the time forbade warships to do. This attention to detail ensured Dewey that his men would have the necessary supplies when they needed them most.

Ensign Hugh Rodman, who served on Dewey's staff, admired Dewey's thoroughness in the same fashion Dewey admired Farragut's. He stated that with Dewey at the helm, "every contingency which might arise was considered and studied, and plans made to meet each one, so that when the time came to engage the enemy's fleet, we had a prearranged plan which fitted the case perfectly."[40]

Dewey realized that attacking Manila, the main Spanish stronghold in the Philippines, would not be easy. Because he was seven thousand miles from the nearest American dockyard, any severely damaged ship would be as good as lost, because it could not be repaired and placed back into battle. In contrast, Spain could handily repair its ships at its own facilities in the Philippines.

Dewey also faced an imposing obstacle at the entrance to Manila Bay. The small islands of Corregidor and Caballo divided the ten-mile-wide entrance to Manila Bay into two narrow channels. Powerful Spanish guns pointed seaward from both islands, ready to unleash a torrent of shells at approaching vessels as they entered either

The Olympia, *Commodore Dewey's flagship, led the U.S. naval fleet in the Pacific.*

channel. If the Spaniards manning those guns were alert and accurate, they could shatter Dewey's force before he had an opportunity to hurl a single shell at the Spanish ships.

Rumors filtered into Hong Kong that the Spanish had mounted powerful guns at Manila and had put in an extensive system of minefields at the opening to the bay. Recalling his experience with Farragut, Dewey discounted the rumors as a Spanish bluff. Dewey only needed the word from Washington to put his plans into effect. On April 24, 1898, Secretary Long cabled the commodore that "War has commenced between the United States and Spain. Proceed at once to Philippine Islands. Commence operations particularly against the Spanish fleet. You must capture vessels or destroy."[41]

Dewey departed Hong Kong that same day. He believed that the quicker he arrived in the Philippines, the greater his chances were of catching the Spanish before their preparations were complete. As the American ships steamed by, observers from European embassies stood on shore to watch the spectacle. Remembering the rumors about Spanish strength in the Philippines, few gave the Americans much chance of emerging victorious. One British official remarked about Dewey's force, "A fine set of fellows, but unhappily we shall never see them again."[42]

SPAIN WAITS FOR DEWEY

Spain commanded considerable military power, but nothing close to what was rumored. Manila's forts sported a large battery of guns. Admiral Don Patricio Montojo y Pasaron, commander of the Spanish naval forces in the Philippines, could have positioned his ships near those guns and taken advantage of the shelter they provided, but he opted to place his ships six miles south of Manila at Cavite, in Canacao Bay inside Manila Bay. Montojo believed he stood little chance of defeating the Americans, and by shifting his ships away from Manila he hoped to spare the city any damage from a bombardment. Somewhat pessimistically, he also believed that his men would have a better chance of surviving if their ships were sunk in the more shallow waters of Canacao Bay.

Montojo arranged his seven ships in a crescent-shaped line from east to west inside Canacao Bay. The cruiser *Reina Cristina*, the outdated wooden cruiser *Castilla*, the small cruisers *Isla de Cuba, Isla de Luzon, Don Antonio de Ulloa,* and *Don Juan de Austria,* and the gunboat *Marques del Duero,* bore thirty-one guns of short range against Dewey's fifty-three, most of which could shoot farther than those of Montojo's fleet. In a standing battle Dewey could theoretically fire from longer ranges than the Spanish guns and inflict damage sooner than his adversary. Similar to Cervera in the Atlantic, Montojo approached the opening of hostilities with an air of resignation about his fate.

TO THE PHILIPPINES

As Dewey's ships headed for the Philippines 620 miles away, sailors tossed wooden items overboard to reduce fire and splinter hazards (wooden sections shattered into hundreds of deadly, razor-sharp pieces when hit by shells). Dewey also asked one

Dewey stands on the Olympia's *bridge as he leads his fleet to the Philippines.*

of the passengers, the American consul to the Philippines, O. F. Williams, to deliver a pep speech to the crew of his flagship, *Olympia.* Williams's fiery oratory stirred the crew to a frenzy when he mentioned Spanish insults to the U.S. flag. He explained that the Spanish considered the Americans an ill-disciplined force and that they boasted that "The struggle will be short and deci-sive. Spain will emerge triumphantly from this new test, humiliating and blasting the adventurers from those States."[43] Upon hearing this, the sailors erupted in scornful laughter and swore to make the Spanish eat their words.

However, Dewey could not expect to surprise the Spanish in Manila. Their consul in Hong Kong had informed them when Dewey left the city, and the Spanish could thus estimate the approximate day of his arrival in Philippine waters. The American commander had little choice but to steam ahead and hope that the tales of superior Spanish defenses were erroneous.

When Dewey neared the entrance to Manila Bay on the afternoon of April 30, he announced to his ranking officers that he intended to lead the ships in that very night instead of waiting until daylight. He predicted that the Spanish would assume Dewey would attack at daybreak, and thus would not be on guard for an immediate attack. He was certain that the Spanish would never expect Dewey to lead his ships through an unfamiliar, unlit channel at night.

When Dewey added that he intended to place the *Olympia* at the head of the line to lead the ships into Manila Bay, his nephew, Lt. William Winder, cautioned that another ship could accept the hazardous position. Dewey declined the advice, telling Winder, "Billy, I have waited sixty years for this opportunity. Mines or no mines, I am leading the squadron in myself."[44]

Montojo Seals His Doom

At this stage Admiral Montojo made a decision that effectively guaranteed his fleet's speedy defeat. Some of his senior commanders wanted him to disperse the Spanish ships throughout the Philippine Islands and force Dewey to hunt down each one. This effort would require weeks to complete, would give Spain more time to prepare on land or to ship reinforcements from Europe, and would spare Manila from bombardment.

Montojo decided against the move. It might have worked had he placed provisions and coal in different harbors throughout the islands, but he had not previously done this. Now there was not enough time. More important, top Spanish political officials in the capital heatedly emphasized that Montojo's ships must remain near Manila to protect Spanish residents in the city.

Montojo thus waited in Canacao Bay inside Manila Bay for Dewey. Even though he knew the American fleet would most likely arrive on May 1, he allowed most of his officers to go ashore the night before instead of requiring them to remain aboard and ready their crews for battle. He doubted his chances of success, so he saw no reason why his officers should not enjoy a final opportunity to relax before they battled the Americans. Unfortunately, this meant that many of his top men were not on station until after the fighting had started.

Into Battle

As darkness settled over the U.S. fleet, American crews manned their battle stations. All lights were extinguished except for a small beacon on the stern [back end] of each ship as a mark for the ships following. Nature lent a helping hand by providing clusters of dark clouds which shrouded the moon.

Dewey put on a tropical white uniform and a golf cap and stepped to his captain's position on the *Olympia*'s bridge, the spot he would occupy for the entire battle. Near midnight the force entered the channel in single file, directly between El Fraile and Caballo Islands. Officers and crew on all ships waited quietly in the dark, expecting the black stillness to explode at any moment in a flurry of Spanish shells or their ship to rock from a mine explosion.

None came, but a sudden glow erupted from the *McCulloch* that petrified every man who could see it. Soot and coal particles in one of the ship's smokestacks had ignited and belched fire into the darkness. The men worried that the Spanish had seen this and would direct a massive bombardment their way.

A correspondent for the *New York World*, Edwin W. Harden, watched the events from his post aboard the *McCulloch*. He wrote in a subsequent story that "There was a grinding of teeth on the *McCulloch*,

for of all times in the world this was the most fatal time for such a thing to happen. While it burned it made a perfect target for the enemy."[45]

Surprisingly, no cannon boomed out an unfriendly greeting. The first four ships passed safely through the channel. Finally, at 12:17 A.M. on May 1, Spanish guns opened fire on the last two vessels, the *Concord* and *Boston*, but their shells splashed harmlessly into the water. Dewey's bold gamble had succeeded in placing his force inside Manila Bay, out of reach of the channel guns. Dewey slowly proceeded toward Manila so he would arrive near the city at daylight. Except for two mines that exploded ahead of the *Olympia*, the journey was uneventful. At

The U.S. fleet sails into Manila Bay to confront the Spanish navy.

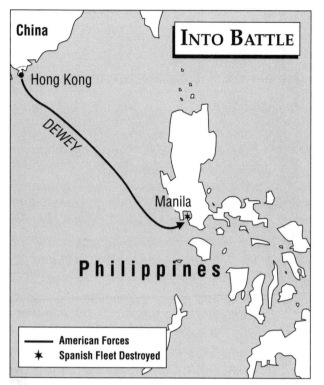

China

INTO BATTLE

Hong Kong

DEWEY

Manila

P h i l i p p i n e s

—— American Forces
★ Spanish Fleet Destroyed

during this time was intense; at any moment a dozen or more men might be scattered about the decks, dead or dying."[46]

When the American force came within five thousand yards of the Spanish, Dewey turned his squadron to the west to parallel the shoreline. He then leaned to the commander of the *Olympia*, Capt. Charles V. Gridley and calmly uttered, "You may fire when you are ready, Gridley."[47] At that command, a shell burst from the *Olympia* signaled the other ships to open fire.

Dewey led his ships in five successive parallel runs across the front of the Spanish fleet, each time raking the enemy with shells. After the first pass, he shortened the range to three thousand yards to improve accuracy. However, some sailors noticed that it also placed them in more danger of being hit by the enemy, whose shells created huge waterspouts in the bay in front of and behind the American fleet and served as deadly reminders that potential injury was only yards away.

Correspondent Harden had a front-row seat for the entire show. His account of the battle included a vivid description of Dewey's five passes.

Our vessels passed along the entire line of ships and forts, firing as rapidly as the guns could be loaded and properly aimed. On they went, in perfect formation, the single line of battle, the port [left side] guns engaging the enemy until the *Olympia* had passed the Sangley Point forts, when she turned

4 A.M. the crews received coffee and hard biscuits at their battle stations.

When Dewey learned that the Spanish fleet had taken station six miles south of Manila at Cavite, he veered his ships in that direction. His own ship, *Olympia*, was followed into battle by the *Baltimore, Raleigh, Petrel, Concord,* and *Boston.* Moving steadily at eight knots toward Cavite, the force came under Spanish fire from Montojo's ships at 5:15 A.M.

Dewey withheld the order to open fire and for more than thirty minutes the American ships steamed directly toward the Spanish while enemy shells burst on all sides. The Spanish scored no hits, but the crews felt intense pressure. Joseph L. Stickney, a war correspondent heading in with the force, wrote that "The strain on the nerves of the crew sharply about, and proceeded down the course again, a little nearer to the shore, bringing her starboard [right side] guns into action. Each ship, as it came to the point where the *Olympia* had turned, swung around, followed into line, and again we passed. Five times our ships went up and down that line, each time with lessened distance, and all the time they kept up a steady, rapid fire upon the enemy.[48]

In spite of the narrowing gap between the opponents, none of the American ships received a single hit. Lieutenant Bradley Fiske marveled that the six vessels slowly steamed back and forth, never once losing their place in line.

The battle turned desperate for the Spanish ships, which had absorbed a string of hits. Desperate to alter the momentum, at 7 A.M. the Spanish *Reina Cristina* charged toward the *Olympia*, but American fire turned the vessel into a battered wreck and killed or wounded half the crew.

On the fourth pass Dewey inched closer to shore and continued firing at the enemy.

American ships bombard enemy ships with shells during the Battle of Manila.

Explosions and fires marked almost every Spanish ship as the shells found their marks. Everything appeared to be going in favor of Dewey, who believed that he only needed to continue the shelling for a while longer before his foe would be knocked out of the battle.

At 7:30, however, Captain Gridley informed him that only fifteen rounds of ammunition remained for the *Olympia*'s big guns, news that astounded the commodore. Dewey had little choice but to order all ships back for a quick check on remaining ammunition, even though the battle appeared to be going favorably. So far, only minor damage had been reported and only eight men had been wounded.

Sailors on every ship, unaware of the shortage, moaned the decision to pull back. The crews were told that the squadron was moving back for breakfast, but most men pleaded to continue the battle. Stickney mentioned that one man begged his commander, "For God's sake, captain, don't let us stop now! To hell with breakfast!" Stickney added, "I do not exaggerate in the least that as we hauled off into the bay, the gloom on the bridge of the *Olympia* was thicker than a London fog in November."[49]

Happily, Dewey learned that the first report had been wrong. Fifteen had been the number of rounds fired, not the amount remaining. The ships returned to action at 11:16 A.M. and focused on reducing the Spanish. Of

Spain's Reina Cristina *is sunk by Americans during the fighting in Manila.*

MONTOJO'S FATE

As was the custom in Spain at the end of the ninteenth century, high-ranking officers who commanded in defeat had to face the condemnation of their superiors. Though Admiral Montojo believed his strategy was correct and contended that his ships were no match for the stronger American unit, he had to argue his case in a court-martial once he returned to Spain. Captain Victor Maria Concas y Palau defended the admiral in his trial, and according to the following account in David F. Trask's The War with Spain in 1898, *Montojo's claims did not prevent punishment from being imposed.*

"He [Montojo] dwelt on the inadequacies of his vessels, guns, and crews, and on the importance of forestalling a bombardment of Manila. Montojo's ships [mostly outdated wooden vessels] were not designed to fight modern ships of the classes included in Dewey's squadron. Concas also stressed the failure of the home government to provide reinforcements. The court-martial convicted Montojo of dereliction of duty, but his sentence was merely to be separated from the service. There were extenuating circumstances; he had fought bravely and sustained a severe wound."

Montojo's ships, only the *Ulloa* could return fire, and the Americans quickly sank it. By 12:30 P.M. a white flag appeared from the Spanish side, indicating that the battle was over.

Dewey gained a lopsided victory. He had destroyed all seven of Montojo's ships, killed 161 crew members, and wounded another 210. Dewey's squadron suffered minor damage—one man perished from heat exhaustion and nine fell with injuries—causing the surgeon aboard the *Raleigh*, Dudley Carpenter, to remark, "To give the devil their due, I must say the Spaniards fought bravely. But they could not shoot straight."[50] The Spanish-American War was barely one week old, and already Spanish naval power in the Pacific had been eliminated.

AFTER THE VICTORY

Because the underwater telegraph cable connecting Manila with Hong Kong had been severed in the action, Dewey could not quickly send word to the United States of his victory. President McKinley and other members of government anxiously awaited information, since they knew that Dewey had gone into battle, but they received no official word for almost one week. Summaries appeared in different newspapers, but they could not be considered accurate until verified by an official report. What frustrated McKinley and the nation was that some stories proclaimed Dewey the victor while others had him pulling back in defeat. The *New York Tribune* printed an article on May 2 which claimed that the U.S.

DEWEY FOR PRESIDENT

Dewey's enormous popularity after the war made him an early contender for the 1900 presidential election. Both parties courted him, and had a national vote been taken immediately after he returned from the Philippines, he might have won. But Dewey proved to be his own worst enemy in the political arena, and two comments sealed his fate. In April 1900 he casually remarked to a newspaper reporter that the office of president required no special skills, because other people performed most of the work. That remark angered citizens throughout the country, who took the comment as demeaning to the chief executive and as an indication that Dewey lacked sufficient knowledge of the office. The next month Dewey lost more support when he explained that he had always been too busy in the military to vote in elections. The brief Dewey for president movement ended as quickly as it had begun.

Dewey's bid for the 1900 presidential election was short-lived.

squadron "inflicted some damage but, suffering considerable loss, withdrew. A second engagement followed, and the U.S. suffered further damage."[51] No one knew what to believe.

Finally, on May 7, McKinley received Dewey's official report proclaiming a glowing victory. The American people exploded in wild displays of patriotism that elevated Dewey and his men to the status of heroes. Parents christened newborn babies "Dewey," and Dewey hats, canes, spoons, and chewing gum—called Dewey's Chewies—filled the tables of merchandise stores. Songwriters penned tunes with titles such as "Dewey's Duty Done" and "What Did Dewey Do to Them," while bartenders could hardly keep pace with demand for a new drink labeled the Manila Punch. Congress quickly promoted the commodore to admiral, and then ten months later further elevated him to Admiral of the Navy, a post never before, or since, granted to a naval officer.

Dewey could not long celebrate in the Philippines, for numerous problems demanded his attention. The Spanish fleet had been removed, but on land the Spanish army still held Manila. Sooner or later that obstacle would have to be faced. Dewey sent a message to Washington stating that he thought he could take the city at any time, but he lacked the forces needed to hold on to it afterward. He notified McKinley that he could "reach no further ashore. For tenure of the land you must have the man with a rifle."[52] More men would have to be sent before action could be taken. In the meantime, Dewey blockaded Manila and waited for reinforcements.

PROBLEMS IN MANILA

Following the triumph in Manila Bay, Dewey embarked on a waiting war. He lacked sufficient forces to land and expel the Spanish from Manila, who outnumbered him twenty to one, so he conducted a blockade of the port city until twenty thousand reinforcements under Maj. Gen. Wesley Merritt arrived from the United States. Since the journey across the Pacific to Manila covered almost eight thousand miles, Merritt would not arrive for two months. Until then, Dewey could do little but enforce the blockade and hope that no help arrived from Spain.

McKinley sent orders that Dewey was not to engage in discussions with Filipino rebel forces, who had gathered near Manila in expectations of assaulting the Spanish army waiting inside the capital. The president preferred to wait until peace negotiations with Spain were completed before handing over any governmental power or control of any land to the Filipino rebels and their leader, Emilio Aguinaldo.

Merritt and the first complement of reinforcements left California on May 25. The next month, with the reinforcements three-fourths of the way to the Philippines, one of Merritt's ships steamed into the island of Guam, a possession of Spain. Spanish officers stationed in the desolate outpost, unaware that war had even been declared between their nation and the United States, came out from shore in two small boats to greet the American vessel. To their surprise and confusion the American officer announced that the Spaniards were now prisoners of war and that Guam belonged to the United States. Possession passed into American hands without a shot being fired.

Much to Dewey's relief, Merritt pulled into Manila Bay on June 30, giving Dewey sufficient strength to take action against the

Major General Wesley Merritt (seated, center) and his forces sailed to the Philippines to help expel the Spanish from Manila.

city of Manila. Throughout July, Dewey sent messages to Spanish officials in Manila in hopes of arranging a peaceful conclusion. When he received no satisfactory reply, Dewey turned to military force.

On August 7 he informed the Spanish governor-general, Fermin Juadenes, that he would bombard the city in forty-eight hours unless he surrendered. Juadenes wanted to hand over the city, but for honor's sake and to satisfy his superiors in Madrid, he could not do so without a fight. Juadenes also worried that once his men laid down their weapons, they would be at the mercy of Filipino rebels.

Dewey and Juadenes arranged a mock battle so the Spaniards could save face. While Dewey promised not to use his large guns against Manila, Juadenes agreed to put up only a show of resistance along the front trenches. A small American force would land near Manila, accept the "surrender" of the Spanish troops, and quickly march into the city. Dewey also promised to post guards around Manila to prevent Filipino rebels from seeking vengeance on their former captors.

The attack unfolded according to plan on August 13. Three American ships fired small shells at one Spanish position while soldiers advanced along the beach. Soon the white flag of surrender appeared above the city wall. American troops now occupied the trenches that had formerly housed the Spanish. Ironically, even though the United States had fought alongside Filipino rebels, they now found themselves surrounded by those same rebels. The fighting against the Spanish had ended, but a more deadly style of warfare was about to begin against Aguinaldo's forces, who were eager to control the destiny of their own nation.

Three days after the fall of Manila, Dewey learned that McKinley had signed a peace agreement with Madrid on August 12—one day before the attack. Had he known of this he could have called off the maneuver and prevented bloodshed. It was to be only the first in a weary string of bloody, unfortunate incidents which marked American fighting in the Philippines.

5 "The Great Day"

While Commodore Dewey guided the American navy to victory in the Pacific, the U.S. Army and Marines organized Cuban invasion forces to defeat the Spanish army stationed in Cuba. In less than three months various units grappled with the Spanish at previously unknown locales, bringing glory to soldiers and officers alike and national renown to Theodore Roosevelt. The events further enhanced the country's reputation as an emerging world power.

MARINES LAND AT GUANTANAMO BAY

The war's first land action unfolded forty miles east of Santiago at Guantanamo Bay on Cuba's southeast coast. The U.S. Navy needed both a coaling station to fuel the large number of ships stationed off the Cuban coast as well as a shelter during the upcoming hurricane season. Top officials hoped the Cuban campaign would end before the weather soured, but in the alternative, they did not want their vessels to be at the mercy of Mother Nature without a safe anchorage.

On June 6 the cruiser *Marblehead* and the auxiliary cruiser *Yankee* headed into the

bay. A lone Spanish gunboat, *Sandoval*, quickly fled the area and was never seen again. American sailors severed a telegraph cable to hamper Spanish communications, then made contact with Cuban rebels ashore. One hundred marines from three other ships—the first American troops to set foot on Cuban soil—then landed to scout the area in preparation for a larger group of marines. On June 10, 648 men of the First Marine Battalion under the command of Lt. Col. Robert W. Huntington established defensive lines, secured a hill beyond the bay, and set up Camp McCalla.

All remained quiet until June 11, when Spanish soldiers attacked and killed two Americans while they ate supper. According to one news correspondent, "From the hills and black shadows of the trees came the sharp crack of the rifles, the bullets thudding on the ground, whirring through the air, chipping off tree branches and leaves, and falling in a hail in the water." [53] Surprised marines, including a small group who had been bathing in the bay, rushed to grab rifles. A string of naked Americans scampered from the water and fell into position along a defensive line set up by Lieutenant Colonel Huntington, hardly worried that they faced the enemy wearing nothing but rifles and their courage. A brief firefight ended with a marine charge that caused the Spanish to abandon their posts. With the skirmish ended, the naked Americans received orders to return to their tents and don uniforms.

The Spanish continued to harass American lines with quick skirmishes and assaults from small units of men, which killed two more marines and wounded three others. One of the casualties, Assistant Surgeon John Blair Gibbs, had just stepped to his tent door and mentioned to companions his fear of dying in Cuba when a Spanish bullet plowed into his forehead and killed him instantly. In response, Capt. George F. Elliot led a force of marines, bolstered by sixty Cuban rebels and gunfire from the gunboat *Dolphin*, against a concentration of Spanish soldiers at nearby Cuzco Well.

During the fighting, Sgt. John H. Wick calmly relayed firing instructions from the marines to the gunboat by standing on an exposed ridge in plain view of the Spanish and waving signal flags to a naval officer aboard the *Dolphin*. Based on Wick's information, the gunboat directed an accurate bombardment against Spanish positions. News correspondent Stephen Crane, who gained fame earlier in his career by writing the classic Civil War novel *The Red Badge of Courage*, cringed close to the ground near Wick to avoid being hit by the flurry of

MARINES AT GUANTANAMO BAY

The U.S. Marine Corps boasts a proud heritage. In some of the nation's most trying moments, members of the Marine Corps have served their country well. During the Spanish-American War a contingent of marines occupied Guantanamo Bay, which was eventually turned into an important American naval and marine base. However, the marines in 1898 received a boost from accompanying reporters. Historian Allan R. Millett relates the following account of the fighting at Guantanamo Bay in his Semper Fidelis: The History of the United States Marine Corps.

"Compared to the fighting soon to follow in the Army's campaign against Santiago, the action at Guantanamo Bay was a minor skirmish of no consequence to the course of the war, but it took on incalculable importance for the Marine Corps. As the first serious fighting by American troops on Cuban soil, it drew a squad of newspaper correspondents. The reporters, among them Stephen Crane [author of *The Red Badge of Courage*], reported the Cuzco Well battle as an epic of bravery and professional skill that proved the military superiority of the Marines. If the Commandant [the top-ranking Marine officer] had staged the campaign for public effect, it could not have been more successful."

Famed American author Stephen Crane chronicled the action at Guantanamo Bay as a news correspondent.

Spanish bullets. Crane later wrote of Wick that "the Spaniards must have concentrated a fire of at least twenty rifles upon him. His society was at that moment sought by none."[54]

The Americans quickly routed the opposition, destroyed the well, and secured the area around Guantanamo Bay. From then on, American supply ships steamed in and out of the bay without interference from Spanish gunfire.

THE ARRIVAL OF THE AMERICAN ARMY

The same week as the action at Guantanamo Bay, Maj. Gen. William R. Shafter, an immense man weighing close to three hundred pounds, received orders from Secretary of War Russell A. Alger to proceed to Santiago, fifty miles west of Guantanamo, and capture or destroy the enemy garrison there. Shafter ordered the first twenty thousand soldiers, including the impatient Roosevelt and his men, aboard steamers on June 8. The ships had barely started for Cuba when word of a possible sighting of the Spanish fleet forced Alger to order a recall. For five sweltering days in the Florida sun, men waited in poorly ventilated holds for the fleet to move again. An irate Roosevelt wrote a friend, "We are in a sewer; a canal which is festering as if it were Havana harbor."[55]

The ships finally departed from Florida on June 14 for the six-day voyage to Cuba. When Shafter arrived, he and Rear Adm. William T. Sampson, commander of naval forces in the operation, argued over where the army should position its troops. Sampson wanted a unit of soldiers to land on each side of Santiago harbor, then attack the Spanish guns which kept his fleet from moving closer to shore. Shafter adamantly rejected this, claiming the assault would cause too many casualties. Instead, he substituted his own plan to land the men fifteen miles east of Santiago at Daiquiri, which was believed to be lightly held. Once ashore, his men would advance to Siboney, only seven miles from Santiago, and prepare for an assault on the port. Shafter had his way.

American troops debark haphazardly after reaching the harbor in Daiquiri.

The operation at Daiquiri soon dissolved into a debacle. Soldiers rode in small landing craft through choppy waters five miles to shore, then had to hop out of their boats onto a rickety wooden pier. If they miscalculated their leap, soldier and equipment splashed into the water or smacked against the pier's concrete pilings.

Army animals experienced an even rougher day. To get the horses ashore, Shafter ordered that they be thrown overboard and allowed to swim to the beach. Some hysterical animals veered out to sea and drowned, but an enterprising bugler on the beach saved most of the horses by sounding a cavalry call. In unison, the horses turned toward shore and swam in.

Theodore Roosevelt lost one of his two horses when the animal drowned in a huge wave as soldiers were carefully hoisting the animal into a boat. A reporter on the scene later wrote that Roosevelt stormed to the spot "snorting like a bull, and split the air with one blasphemy after another."[56] Taking more care with Roosevelt's second horse, named Texas, the soldiers landed the animal without mishap. A calmer Roosevelt, with several pairs of extra spectacles sewn into the lining of his hat, left for the beach to join the Rough Riders.

Most men were anxious to engage the Spanish. Little had yet occurred to sully their views of fighting—no blood had been shed, no limbs severed, no deaths recorded. "Fighting Joe" Wheeler, the former Confederate officer, typified the reaction of most, even though he named the wrong enemy when he blurted that he could not wait to get a crack at "the Yankees—dammit, I mean the Spaniards."[57]

THE ROAD TO SAN JUAN

The Spanish army commander in Cuba, Gen. Arsenio Linares, had ten thousand soldiers at his disposal in Santiago, but he immediately tossed away his advantage in numbers by dispersing the men in a series of strong points instead of concentrating them along the only jungle route available to the Americans. While the Spanish officer hoped to delay the Americans long enough for Cuba's natural allies—yellow fever and dysentery—to take their toll, he ignored one of the military's most basic tenets. Linares could have enjoyed a two-to-one edge in numbers had he kept his forces together, but fortunately for General Shafter, the way the Spanish were positioned allowed Shafter to methodically attack each stronghold along the path.

Shafter was eager to get his men going as quickly as possible. Cuba's rainy season, frequently interrupted with ferocious hurricanes and lashing winds, was due to start any day, and Shafter knew that it was only a matter of time before disease reduced his numbers.

On June 23, 1898, two regiments under the command of Gen. Henry W. Lawton left the beaches and headed toward Siboney, a town seven miles away which Shafter assumed housed Spanish soldiers. They cautiously approached, but to their surprise found the place deserted.

The Americans paused for a few days to regroup and allow time for needed supplies to reach them. The supply system, however, could not move equipment rapidly along the solitary path, which was little more than a trail hacked out of the jungle. Food and ammunition piled up on the beaches while only a trickle of material arrived at the front. "It was simply to get the bare necessities of life to those men," said Shafter, "and it taxed them to the utmost, the pack trains and all—the bare bread and sugar and coffee."[58]

Despite the supply problems, confident American soldiers stood ready to enter battle with their opposition. One group of officers held up glasses of whiskey and toasted, "To the Officers—may they get killed, wounded or promoted!"[59]

On the other side of the lines the Spanish seemed equally confident. These battle-tested troops waited in well-fortified trenches and guardhouses shielded by barbed wire. A newspaper in Spain informed its readers, "The average height among the Americans is five feet two inches. This is due to their living almost entirely upon vegetables as they ship all their beef out of the country, so eager are they to make money. There is no doubt that one full-grown Spaniard can defeat any three men in America."[60]

ACTION AT LAS GUASIMAS AND EL CANEY

The Spanish would soon have to take back their words. On June 24, American units advanced in single file toward Las Guasimas, where information indicated that fifteen hundred Spaniards waited. Sergeant Hamilton Fish, son of a prominent politician, and Capt. Allyn Capron Jr. took the advance position (the point) a short distance ahead of the Rough Riders. Toward the rear stood Theodore Roosevelt and his commanding

A Father and His Son

One of the more touching moments during the war involved Capt. Allyn Capron, Jr., who died in the fighting at Las Guasimas. Following the battle the bodies of eight slain Americans were hastily buried in a communal gravesite to keep the remains safe from vultures and land crabs. The soldiers who buried the men, however, had no time to place a marker listing the bodies resting beneath the soil. As other soldiers passed by the unmarked grave on their way to combat, they could hardly pause to say a prayer, but one man filtered over for a quiet moment of reflection. He had been informed that Captain Capron's remains reposed at the spot. The man, Capt. Allyn Capron, Sr., battery commander of the Fourth Artillery and father of the slain officer, stood for a few moments absorbed with his own thoughts. He then turned to the road and headed on toward the fighting.

Captain Allyn Capron Jr. died in battle at Las Guasimas.

officer, Col. Leonard Wood, accompanied by newspaper correspondents Richard Harding Davis of the *New York Herald* and Edward Marshall of the *New York Journal*.

Suddenly the jungle came alive. Bullets whizzed through leaves, thudded into trees and the ground, and ripped into Rough Riders. Sergeant Fish dropped dead in the opening seconds, and a bullet shattered Capron's heart an instant after that. Six other Rough Riders perished a few moments later as men huddled for cover.

The Rough Riders took shelter in the thick jungle so hastily that Roosevelt feared he would lose touch with his men. Correspon-

dent Davis wrote that entering the foreboding canopy was "like forcing the walls of a maze. If each trooper had not kept in touch with the man on either hand he would have been lost in the thicket."[61]

They tried to locate the origin of the firing, but because the Spanish used a smokeless powder, no white trace lingered to indicate where they were hidden. Thirty-four more Rough Riders lay wounded, including a soldier named Private Isbell, who was hit three times in the neck, twice in the left hand, and once in the right hand and forehead. Roosevelt courageously stood in the midst of the action directing return fire and somehow avoiding the deadly bullets, although one struck a tree only inches from his cheek and splattered splinters of bark into his face.

Finally, Davis spotted a line of Spaniards on the summit of a nearby hill. Roosevelt directed the Rough Riders to concentrate their fire at that point, and a barrage of American bullets soon forced the Spaniards to flee. At that moment nine hundred American soldiers, including the Rough Riders and troops of the all African American Tenth Cavalry, charged the Spanish positions. The Rough Riders swerved to the Spanish right flank and rear while the Tenth Calvary charged directly at the Spanish lines. Roosevelt and the Rough Riders gained the top of the hill outside of Las Guasimas and ended the brief encounter.

Following the seizure of Las Guasimas, Shafter turned his attention to the second of Linares's three defensive lines. This one ran through the village of El Caney and the ridges of two hills in front of Santiago—San Juan Hill and Kettle Hill. Six miles northeast of Santiago, El Caney featured six wooden blockhouses and one stone fort manned by 520 soldiers. Before Shafter could seize San Juan Hill, the last obstacle before Santiago, he had to eliminate El Caney.

His plan was to have General Lawton attack El Caney with one infantry division. Shafter figured that Lawton could take the village in two hours, at which time Lawton's men would turn to their left and join the subsequent attack against San Juan and Kettle Hills. Shafter intended to commence

The African American troops of the Tenth Cavalry charge the Spanish at Las Guasimas.

WOUNDED CORRESPONDENT

To provide real-life coverage of war for their readers, newspaper writers ate the same food, slept in the same tents, and headed toward the same battlefields as the troops about whom they wrote. Correspondent Edward Marshall of the New York Journal *covered the fighting at Las Guasimas with Theodore Roosevelt when he heard a smack and felt himself falling to the ground. G. J. A. O'Toole's* The Spanish War *includes a description of the event by Marshall, who survived his wound.*

"There was no pain, no surprise. The tremendous shock so dulled my sensibilities that it did not occur to me that anything extraordinary had happened. I merely lay perfectly satisfied and entirely comfortable in the long grass."

the action before thirty-six hundred Spanish reinforcements arrived in Santiago and bolstered Linares's lines.

Shafter, hoping for supplies to arrive, waited six days before issuing the orders to move forward. Linares took advantage of that respite to strengthen his defensive lines at every location.

On July 1, which Roosevelt later described as "the great day of my life,"[62] Lawton's sixty-six hundred men advanced toward the blockhouses at 6:30 A.M. The drive quickly stalled when they encountered barbed wire and deadly gunfire. For eight hours the Americans futilely attempted to advance before a break occurred. As usually happens in battle, individual initiative swerves the fighting one way or the other. In this instance two privates, James W. Smith and James L. McMillen, crept toward the barbed wire and, with bullets screaming by, cut the wire with pliers.

This opened the floodgates for a general assault toward Spanish trenches and blockhouses. Gatling machine guns helped pin down the Spanish defenders, and many a man foolish enough to raise his head above the top of his trench for a glimpse of the American charge slumped to the bottom with a bullet hole in his forehead. American troops rushed to the top, grappled with the remaining Spanish soldiers, and seized the blockhouses.

The sight at the blockhouses made an indelible impression on American fighting men. Captain Arthur H. Lee stepped inside the fort and recalled that

the halls were splashed with blood and a dozen dead and wounded were laid out on the floor, or wedged under the debris. The trench around the fort was a gruesome sight, floored with dead Spaniards in horribly contorted attitudes and with sightless, staring eyes. Others were littered about the slope, and these were mostly terribly mutilated by shell fire. Those killed in the trenches were all shot through the forehead, and their brains oozed out like white paint from a color-tube.[63]

Although the U.S. Army enjoyed another victory, it had absorbed stiff losses. For ten hours a smaller Spanish force had held up the Americans and killed or wounded almost 450 men. Roosevelt and others worried that if El Caney proved this difficult, how much harder would the defenses be directly in front of Santiago?

PRELUDE TO SAN JUAN

Later that day Shafter ordered ten thousand Americans to move against the final two Spanish-held hills. They would not have an easy time. In stifling heat that eventually rose

General Shafter's troops fiercely assault the Spanish fortifications at El Caney.

to one hundred degrees, the American soldiers had to ford a stream under enemy fire, then head along a road winding between the two hills. To their left loomed the larger San Juan Hill while the smaller Kettle Hill was to the right. While Gen. Jacob F. Kent led the advance toward San Juan Hill, in a supporting action Roosevelt's Rough Riders and the African American Ninth Cavalry were to eliminate the Spanish at Kettle Hill, then join Kent's larger assault on San Juan.

Wood and Roosevelt gathered the Rough Riders and started to file along the road, accompanied by the Ninth Cavalry, when three shells suddenly burst above their heads. Roosevelt recalled,

> there was a peculiar whistling, singing sound in the air. From the second shell one of the shrapnel [pieces of sharp metal produced by a shell's explosion] bullets dropped on my wrist, hardly breaking the skin, but raising a bump about as big as a hickory nut. The same shell wounded four of my regiment, and two or three of the regulars were also hit, one losing his leg by a great fragment of shell.[64]

Spanish snipers added to the noise. Four bullets tore open one Rough Rider from his thigh to his knee. A popular officer, Capt. William O. "Bucky" O'Neill, who contended that an officer should never take cover because his job was to instill courage in the men, casually strolled among the soldiers exhorting them to take the attack to the enemy. His men begged him to get down, and one sergeant warned, "Captain, a bullet is sure to hit you."

O'Neill laughed, puffed on the cigarette that always seemed to be dangling from his mouth, and replied, "Sergeant, [a] Spanish bullet isn't made that will kill me."[65] As O'Neill turned to look to the side, a bullet struck him in the mouth and exited the back of his head, instantly killing him.

The slaughter was compounded when the Rough Riders and Ninth Cavalry had to wade across the San Juan River in plain view of the enemy on San Juan and Kettle Hills. Bodies piled up so rapidly that men later labeled the location Bloody Ford. More than four hundred Americans died or were wounded along the trail and at the river.

For over an hour the officers at the front seemed confused. Shafter assumed that his men would continue to charge across the field of waist-high grass toward the enemy

Captain William O. "Bucky" O'Neill was killed by snipers en route to Kettle Hill.

Roosevelt (far right) led the Rough Riders to victory at Kettle Hill.

fortifications, but most officers were waiting for additional orders. After this stalemate had stretched on for ninety long minutes, Roosevelt took matters into his own hands. He remarked to an associate that the men could not long remain where they were without being wiped out, and that the only thing to do was to get up and go after the enemy.

Sitting atop his horse Texas, Roosevelt turned to his men and shouted, "Are you afraid to stand up when I am on horseback?"[66] They rose from their hiding spots and formed a line behind Roosevelt. Alternately offering words of encouragement and swearing at the men to continue, Roosevelt took the Rough Riders and the Ninth

Cavalry to the open field and veered right toward Kettle Hill.

Midway up the hill a shell fragment glanced off Roosevelt's arm and inflicted a small wound, but the indomitable leader continued on. "By this time," he later wrote in his account of the war, "we were all in the spirit of the thing and greatly excited by the charge, the men cheering and running forward between shots."[67]

Forty yards from the summit Roosevelt encountered barbed wire and leapt off Texas. He and his orderly, Pvt. Henry Bardshar, ran ahead of the others, shooting and yelling. Roosevelt watched as Bardshar fired at two Spaniards, who fell to the ground. As a handful of remaining Spanish soldiers fled, the two men reached Kettle Hill's summit, then turned to see the rest of the Rough Riders and the Ninth Cavalry swarming up the slopes.

CLIMAX AT SAN JUAN

Triumphant at Kettle Hill, Roosevelt glanced toward the action on nearby San Juan Hill, where Kent's infantry appeared to be having great difficulty moving against lethal Spanish fire from the trenches and the blockhouse. The thousand or so Spanish soldiers on San Juan knew that the Americans had to exit the jungle from one or both of two trails that led onto the plains in front of the hill. Every rifle and piece of artillery targeted those exits, and when Kent's men filtered to the plains they met a withering hail of fire that cut them down.

Soldiers stumbled forward in the waist-high grass to seek whatever shelter they could find. One soldier wrote that "the heat from the sun was almost unbearable, and quite a number of men, officers and enlisted, fell on the way from its effects, and all the while the Spaniards were throwing volley after volley into us, and men of every rank fell at each volley."[68]

Another trooper recalled the horror that many men felt at being trapped in such an exposed position, with shells crashing overhead and bullets spitting pieces of turf and wads of grass into the air. "It seemed that if one stuck out his hand, the fingers would be clipped off. We huddled within ourselves and bent over to shield our bellies. Overhead, a shell burst—like the popping of a blown-up paper bag."[69]

Gradually, enough soldiers started firing back at the Spanish trenches to permit intermittent advances. When Gatling machine guns arrived later in the afternoon the momentum swung to the Americans, who charged up the final seven hundred yards to the hill's crest.

Lieutenant Jules Ord, saber in hand, raced ahead of one group of Americans and urged them to follow. The advance up the

Soldiers of the Tenth Cavalry charge toward the opposition at San Juan Hill.

hillside turned into an unorganized sprint conducted by hundreds of small units hustling up the slopes. Rough Riders streaming over from Kettle Hill, Regular Army soldiers, and African American troops became intermingled as they advanced toward the top. Ord never halted until he hit the summit, where he and his men defeated the few remaining enemy soldiers. Sadly, Ord was killed before the battle ended.

Roosevelt was more fortunate. As the battle raged, he and Henry Bardshar sprinted across the plain and up the side of San Juan Hill to the Spanish fortifications. When Roosevelt neared the trenches, according to his account of the battle, "two Spaniards leapt from the trenches and fired at us, not ten yards away. As they turned to run I closed in and fired twice, missing the first and killing the second."[70] The remaining Spanish troops abandoned their trenches and fled toward Santiago.

Since the action at San Juan Hill, involved more troops than Kettle Hill and eliminated tougher Spanish positions, the two actions have frequently been combined into one or confused as the same action. Consequently, Theodore Roosevelt became known as the hero of San Juan Hill, even though he performed his most courageous acts of leadership at Kettle Hill. Roosevelt astutely parlayed this reputation into a political career that began as governor of New York and culminated as president of the United

States. July 1 proved, indeed, to be a great day for Theodore Roosevelt.

The Americans paid dearly for removing the final Spanish defense lines blocking the way to Santiago. The actions cost the United States 205 dead and 1,180 wounded, while the Spanish suffered 215 dead and 376 wounded.

As American soldiers stood on San Juan's crest and peered down at Santiago and its harbor, they spotted the fleet of Admiral Cervera bobbing at anchor. The U.S. Army had chased the Spaniards into Santiago, and now their counterparts in the U.S. Navy had to deal with Cervera. The subsequent naval battle off Santiago was the culmination of actions taken by Admiral Sampson since the war's beginning.

6 Spain's Defeat

From the moment he received orders to take the Spanish squadron across the Atlantic to Santiago, Admiral Cervera held few hopes that he could successfully grapple with the American fleet. He knew, though, that he would one day have to steam into battle against his superior foe. Now that the American army had shattered General Linares's lines of defense anchored at El Caney, Kettle Hill, and San Juan Hill, Cervera's frightening moment had arrived. His subsequent actions ended a three-month series of naval encounters in the Caribbean that started in April and led to Spain's defeat.

The Blockade Takes Effect

The blockade of Cuba produced the first naval battles. On April 22 an American cruiser fired a shot over the bow of the Spanish merchant ship *Buenaventura*, which was ferrying lumber from Mississippi to Europe, as a sign for it to halt. Some of the cruiser's sailors then took possession of the Spanish vessel and crew and headed to Key West.

Action intensified on May 11 when the unprotected cruiser *Marblehead* and the gunboat *Nashville* arrived off Cienfuegos to cut the telegraph lines that connected Spanish

officials in Cuba with the outside world. Sailors and marines boarded small boats, headed for the cables, and began to sever the three lines of communication. But heavy enemy fire wounded nine men and forced the unit to leave, with one cable still operating.

Commander Bowman H. McCalla, the officer in charge of the cable-cutting effort, praised his men for doing their best while under deadly fire. "Their work was performed with utmost coolness and intrepidity under most trying circumstances,"[71] concluded McCalla in his official report. Two of the nine wounded later died from their injuries.

On that same day the U.S. torpedo boat *Winslow*, the gunboat *Wilmington*, and the revenue cutter *Hudson* attempted to capture Spanish warships at anchor in Cárdenas, a port eighty miles east of Havana. As the *Winslow* moved closer to shore a Spanish shell hit it and disabled one engine, jammed the rudder, and damaged the steering gear. Lieutenant John B. Bernadou, the ship's commander, finally extricated the vessel by alternately heading forward and back in a zigzag course that slowly took the ship away from shore. While five members of the crew died and three suffered wounds in the short encounter, the Spanish ships were so damaged that they were no longer a factor in the war.

HUNT FOR THE SPANISH NAVY

While the U.S. Navy concentrated on tightening the blockade, Spanish admiral Cervera attempted to dash into Cuba without being sighted. On April 29 the Spanish fleet left the Cape Verde Islands off Africa's western coast. Sampson learned of the departure and guessed that Cervera would head to Puerto Rico first, so he took most of his ships to that island five hundred miles east of Cuba. Sampson arrived on May 12 but found no sign of his foe. Because instead of going to Puerto Rico, Cervera had swerved southeast to the island of Martinique off the South American coast, then sprinted to Curaçao, slightly north of Venezuela.

A frustrated Sampson returned to Cuban waters to tighten the naval blockade. While Commodore Winfield Scott Schley's force watched Cienfuegos on Cuba's southern coast, Sampson headed north to block Havana. Sampson concluded that the Spanish admiral had to enter one or the other location, but once again Cervera outfoxed Sampson. Cervera snuck into the unguarded port of Santiago on Cuba's southern coast, 360 miles southeast of Cienfuegos and 500 miles from Havana.

American sailors spotted Cervera's fleet at anchor a few days later. By June 1 an embarrassed U.S. Navy had ships stationed off Santiago to prevent Cervera from leaving. For the next month the two fleets sat within miles of each other, bobbing at anchor either inside the port or barely outside. Sampson longed to do battle with the Spanish, but he hesitated going directly into the harbor because that would require passing

The U.S. torpedo boat Winslow *suffered extensive damage after a Spanish shell hit and disabled an engine.*

by large Spanish cannons in coastal fortifications. Since the entrance to Santiago's harbor was so narrow, only one ship at a time could enter the channel. This would give Spanish cannoneers a golden opportunity to destroy Sampson's force piecemeal. Sampson thus had to wait until U.S. ground forces, due to arrive soon, attacked the forts and removed the threat posed by the coastal artillery.

Although Cervera could not inflict much damage to the superior American fleet, his mere presence in Cuban waters affected Sampson. The American admiral had hoped to speed across the Atlantic to bombard Spanish coastal waters once the blockade had taken effect, but he could not afford to leave while Cervera's ships posed a menace in Cuba. Also, Sampson could not risk leaving and permitting Cervera to emerge from an unguarded Santiago and attack the East Coast. Should that occur Sampson would face a hasty end to his career.

GUTS AND GLORY IN SANTIAGO HARBOR

In order to solve these problems, Sampson devised a plan to permanently confine Cervera to the harbor. Since only one narrow channel wound into the bay, Sampson concluded that one ship sunk there in the proper location could block any vessel from entering or leaving Santiago Bay.

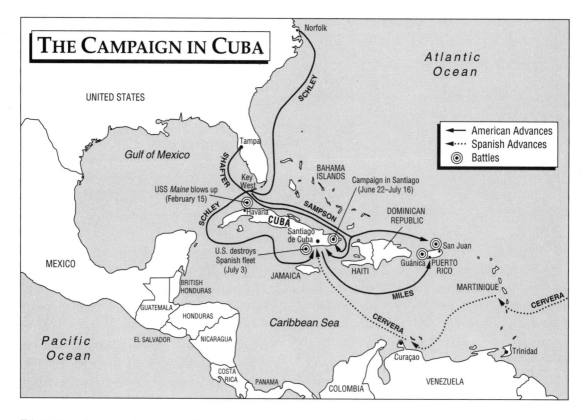

THE CAMPAIGN IN CUBA

Atlantic Ocean

UNITED STATES

Norfolk

SCHLEY

Tampa

Gulf of Mexico

SHAFTER

Key West

SCHLEY

USS *Maine* blows up (February 15)

Havana

CUBA

Santiago de Cuba

BAHAMA ISLANDS

Campaign in Santiago (June 22–July 16)

SAMPSON

DOMINICAN REPUBLIC

San Juan

MEXICO

U.S. destroys Spanish fleet (July 3)

JAMAICA

HAITI

Guánica

PUERTO RICO

MILES

MARTINIQUE

CERVERA

BRITISH HONDURAS

GUATEMALA

HONDURAS

EL SALVADOR

NICARAGUA

Caribbean Sea

CERVERA

Curaçao

Trinidad

Pacific Ocean

COSTA RICA

PANAMA

COLOMBIA

VENEZUELA

American Advances
Spanish Advances
Battles

Admiral William Sampson commanded the North Atlantic fleet.

This would require men to take a ship to the correct location, anchor it in spot, and detonate explosives on board so it would settle to the bottom—all while under heavy enemy fire from shore. In spite of the danger posed by the near-suicidal mission, every member of the battleship *Iowa*—six hundred officers and men—volunteered. Since Capt. Robley D. Evans could only choose one man to represent his ship, he used a coin toss to determine the "winner." The selected seaman received bids as high as fifty dollars to yield his spot in the mission, but he declined all offers.

Under the command of Naval Constructor Richmond Pearson Hobson, seven men gathered on the collier *Merrimac*. As Hobson led the ship toward the channel's entrance in total darkness at about 3 A.M. on June 3, Spanish shells splashed uncomfortably close, but the inaccurate shots missed their target. The *Merrimac* chugged into the channel, where Hobson halted the engines and allowed the ship to slowly drift into place.

Back at the fleet, anxious officers and men knew from the sounds of gunshots that Hobson had been sighted by the Spanish. Correspondent W. A. M. Goode reported that the flash of guns lit the darkness

> and in a few seconds the mouth of Santiago harbor was livid with flames that shot viciously from both banks, and then we knew that the *Merrimac* had been discovered. The dull sound of the cannonade and its fiery light were unmistakable evidences of the fierce attack that was being waged upon Hobson's gallant crew. Whether that vessel had been sunk before she gained the entrance of the harbor, or whether she had been successful, were questions we were utterly unable to answer.[72]

Hobson and his seven companions ignored the Spanish bullets and hastily set up the string of explosives. Unfortunately, when Spanish fire disabled the *Merrimac's* steering gear, Hobson could do little to control the ship. He let it float until he was near the desired spot, then dropped both anchors and detonated the charges, but only two of the ten charges exploded. When one of the anchors failed to hold, the *Merrimac* drifted out of control toward a deeper, wider portion of the entrance, where it began sinking.

Spanish fire enveloped the hapless ship and trapped the eight Americans. Hobson later recalled:

HOBSON THE HERO

The attempt by Richmond Hobson to block Santiago harbor did not succeed, but some journalists glossed over that detail so they could print the types of stories they knew their readers wanted. Commodore Dewey had already captured the nation's attention, and this unheralded naval officer Hobson would be the next, even if it meant altering the facts. Allan Keller includes the following in his Spanish-American War: A Compact History:

"What they [the reporters] did not know did not stop many of the correspondents from filing stories back home indicating that the attempt had been a success. Using the fanciest adjectives in their vocabularies, they told of the heroism of the formerly unsung naval constructor, and before the day was over the people of the United States had a new hero—Richmond Pearson Hobson. It was the sort of news Americans had been waiting to hear. Dewey's victory had grown a little stale, and nothing is more desirable than a hero in war time. Now there was a new one."

All firing was at point-blank range, at a target that could hardly be missed. The striking projectiles produced a grinding sound, with a fine ring in it of steel on steel. The deck vibrated heavily, and we felt the full effect, lying as we were, full-length on our faces. At each instant it seemed that certainly the next would bring a projectile among us.[73]

The seven volunteers pleaded with Hobson to lead them off the doomed vessel, but Hobson dismissed the move as foolhardy. If they left their place of concealment on the ship to jump overboard, they would certainly be seen by the Spanish and come under a more devastating fire. The proper move, in his opinion, was to remain on the *Merrimac* until the ship sank.

Cast into the water by the sinking vessel, the eight Americans gathered around some of the ship's debris and floated among the ruins. Spanish boats crisscrossed the waters in the dark, vainly attempting to find the enemy men, but Hobson's group evaded capture. As dawn broke, Hobson finally concluded that they could not long remain in the chilly waters or elude their foe, so Hobson called out to a passing Spanish boat.

Hobson's hopes of surrendering appeared dim when he spotted a group of riflemen aboard the launch readying their weapons. He shouted across the water that they wanted to surrender, and asked if an officer was aboard. A regal-looking man suddenly appeared, waved off the soldiers with a brisk movement of his hand, and beckoned to the weary Americans. Hobson and his compatriots swam toward the launch, climbed aboard, and found that the officer who had allowed them to surrender was none other than Admiral Cervera. The Spanish commander sent word to the Americans that he had the eight men in custody, that they were free of injury, and that they would be well treated.

Hobson's attempt had failed, but news correspondents turned him and his seven companions into heroes. Articles boasted of their bravery. One story labeled Hobson's feat "a single deed of magnificent American daring"[74] that ranked with John Paul Jones's and other fabled American naval heroics.

A LOST SQUADRON

Meanwhile, because of the unfavorable fortunes in the land battles suffered at the hands of the American army, which culminated in San Juan Hill, on July 2 the highest-ranking Spanish official in Cuba, Governor-General Ramon Blanco, ordered Cervera to leave Santiago harbor as quickly as possible, even if it meant certain destruction at the hands of Admiral Sampson's blockading ships. Blanco believed that such an action was far more honorable than allowing his ships to be destroyed at their anchorages or taken by the Americans. Cervera, feeling the weight of responsibility for his two thousand men, hoped to avoid useless bloodshed and argued that if he remained in the harbor, his sailors could help defend the city. He added that the guns on his ships could also be dismounted and sent to the front lines to be used against the American advance.

Blanco gave him no alternative. Cervera readied his vessels for the open sea, where some thought he might be able to outrun the American ships. However, the admiral realized the foolishness of that viewpoint. His ships had been in poor shape before arriving in Cuba, and in the interlude the hulls had further deteriorated. Besides, the Spanish ships contained too much flammable wood in their designs, and with the fighting around Santiago, Cervera had not had the opportunity to adequately train his crews.

The despondent officer wrote to General Linares about his ominous situation. "I have considered the squadron lost ever since it left Cape Verde, for to think anything else seems madness to me in view of the enormous disparity which exists between our own forces and those of the enemy."[75]

On July 3, Admiral Cervera led his six ships out of Santiago harbor. Steaming six hundred yards apart, the ships emerged from the harbor at ten-minute intervals. The flagship *Maria Teresa*, with Admiral Cervera

Admiral Cervera's troops prepare to leave Santiago harbor to confront American naval forces.

aboard, appeared first, followed by the other three cruisers, *Vizcaya, Cristobal Colon*, and *Almirante Oquendo*, and the two torpedo boat destroyers, *Pluton* and *Furor*.

As the ships headed toward the high seas, Capt. Victor Maria Concas y Palau of the *Maria Teresa* ordered bugles sounded to announce the start of action. Concas, who also understood the gravity of the situation, turned to Cervera and exclaimed, "Poor Spain!" He added that "The sound of my bugles was the signal that the history of four centuries of grandeur was at an end and that Spain was becoming a nation of the fourth class."[76]

"GO RIGHT FOR THEM!"

Cervera's American counterpart, Admiral Sampson, was not even in the area when the Spanish fleet left Santiago harbor. He had taken a unit of three ships to Siboney farther down the coast for a conference with General Shafter. In Sampson's absence, Commodore Winfield Scott Schley aboard the armored cruiser *Brooklyn* assumed command. With him were the four battleships *Indiana, Oregon, Iowa*, and *Texas*, the armed yacht *Vixen*, and an assortment of smaller vessels.

Schley quickly spotted Cervera. Schley asked a lieutenant to make sure Sampson had not returned, and when that had been determined he set about directing the American response. When a lieutenant standing near Schley shouted that the Spanish were steaming directly at the *Brooklyn*, Schley boldly said, "Go right for them!"[77]

The *Maria Teresa* charged out of the harbor in plain view of the *Brooklyn* in an effort to

Commodore Winfield Scott Schley led the naval assault against Cervera's fleet.

head west and outrun the Americans. When the vessels were six hundred yards apart, the *Brooklyn* swerved hard to starboard [right] and cut in front of the *Texas*. The stunned captain of the battleship had to reverse engines to avoid a collision, which put the ship out of the battle for the moment. Other commanders who watched the *Brooklyn*'s movements were appalled that Schley had allowed the ship to veer away from an enemy, but Schley later answered that he swerved to starboard to evade what he thought was a ramming maneuver by the *Maria Teresa*. In the meantime, the commanders had turned their ships to port [left] to pursue the Spanish.

Cervera's flagship suffered the battle's first wounds. Two shells from the *Iowa* ripped in succession into the *Maria Teresa*. The first shell burst steam pipes and sprayed hot steam belowdecks that either instantly scalded sailors to death or flattened them on the deck with horrific burns. The second shell ignited fires throughout the wooden vessel.

Cervera realized that his ship was doomed, and to prevent further loss of life he ordered the *Maria Teresa* run aground. As flames engulfed the ship, Cervera supervised an orderly abandonment and remained aboard until every other Spanish sailor and officer had departed.

A few hundred yards away the captain and crew of the *Iowa* watched the results of their bombardment. The sailors emitted a tremendous cheer as the flames grew larger. Captain Robley D. Evans recalled,

It was a magnificent, sad sight to see these beautiful ships in their death agonies; but we were doing the work we had been educated for, and we cheered and yelled until our throats were sore.[78]

The dying and maiming continued elsewhere as well. The American fleet hotly pursued the *Furor* and *Pluton* and reduced them to burning wrecks in the shark-infested waters. At least fifty shells from American ships hammered the *Almirante Oquendo*. As it was run aground, sailors aboard the pursuing *Texas* lustily cheered. Unlike Evans on the *Iowa*, Capt. John W. Philip quieted his men. "Don't cheer, men; those poor fellows are dying."[79]

Only two Spanish ships remained afloat. Schley's *Brooklyn* closed in on the *Vizcaya* and they engaged in a brief duel, reminiscent of

The battleship Brooklyn *nearly collided with another American ship to avoid being rammed by a Spanish ship.*

The American and Spanish fleets battle in Santiago Bay.

two western gunfighters shooting it out at close range. One Spanish shell demolished a gun compartment and wounded one sailor, while American shells rocked and battered the *Vizcaya* so badly that its sailors were tossed into the air. On the *Brooklyn*, members of a gun crew heard Chief Yeoman George Ellis call out the distances when they heard a sickening *thud!* Blood and brains splattered the men near Ellis, who had been decapitated by a shell. His companions started to lift the headless body over the ship's side so the rest of the crew would not be demoralized by the sight, but Schley ordered them to take Ellis's remains below to be buried later. Finally, hit by so many shells that the vessel

could no longer run under its own steam, the *Vizcaya* ran aground eighteen miles from Santiago.

Rather than throw away his men's lives in a hopeless cause, the captain of the lone Spanish ship afloat, the *Cristobal Colon*, ran the vessel aground fifty miles west of Santiago. With her loss, the lopsided Battle of Santiago Bay ended in a resounding American victory.

DEFEAT OF THE SPANISH NAVY

In the battle's aftermath, American vessels stopped to rescue Spanish sailors swimming in the water or clinging to debris. Captain

SCHLEY

Winfield Scott Schley was born in Frederick County, Maryland, in 1839. After graduating from the Naval Academy at Annapolis in 1860, Schley served in the Civil War. He then taught at the Naval Academy before heading to the Far East as part of the navy's small contingent there. Schley drew praise for his 1884 expedition that rescued survivors trapped in northern Greenland. Five years later he became the commanding officer of the cruiser *Baltimore*.

When the war started, Schley, by then a commodore, commanded a naval squadron responsible for protecting the American eastern seaboard from attack by Admiral Cervera. When the Spanish admiral was blocked inside Santiago harbor, Schley led his force to Cuba to join with Rear Adm. William T. Sampson.

Schley retired from the navy in 1901 bitter over the dispute with Sampson over who should receive credit for the victory at Santiago. He died ten years later.

Schley (fourth from left) stands with members of the expedition that rescued survivors trapped in northern Greenland.

Evans of the *Iowa* moved his ship into position to help a group of Spaniards who, while they attempted to dodge bullets fired by Cuban rebels ashore, also tried to fend off a circling pack of sharks. One of the men picked up was the wounded Capt. Antonio Eulate of the *Vizcaya*. When he came aboard the *Iowa*, Evans had his marines stand at attention and ordered his officer of the deck to salute the Spanish commander. In the grand tradition of warfare, the defeated Eulate offered his sword to the victorious Evans, who readily declined. As the American crew cheered, Evans grasped Eulate's hand and said, "Keep your sword, sir. You have fought like a brave and gallant sailor." [80]

Evans later received the rescued Admiral Cervera and offered him the same respectful treatment given Eulate. Evans recalled that the opposing admiral had maintained his dignity even in defeat.

> As the distinguished officer stepped onto the quarterdeck, the crew of the *Iowa* broke out into cheers, and for fully a minute Admiral Cervera stood bowing his thanks. It was the recognition of gallantry by brave men, and the recipient was fully aware of its meaning. Though he was scantily clad, bareheaded, and without shoes, he was an Admiral every inch of him. [81]

The kindness shown by the Americans touched the Spanish officers and men, who thanked their captors for their graciousness. As Captain Eulate was being taken to a cabin on the *Iowa*, he turned toward his sinking ship, *Vizcaya*, and shouted a farewell. At that moment an explosion rocked the vessel,

and the stricken ship disappeared beneath the waves.

In less than four hours Spain incurred 323 dead, 151 wounded, and the loss of every ship in the battle off Santiago Bay. The remaining men—1,720—became prisoners of war. In contrast, the United States suffered one death—George Ellis—and one wounded. One of the few negative aspects from an American point of view was their sailors' poor marksmanship. A post-battle study indicated that Schley's ships fired a combined 9,433 rounds at the Spanish, but only 123 of them hit their targets.

Captain Evans and his men salute the defeated Admiral Cervera as he boards the Iowa.

Spanish officials found the defeat a bitter pill to swallow, but they did their best to hide their disappointment. A public notice of the battle posted in many locations throughout Cuba stated that

Fortune does not always favor the brave. The Spanish squadron, under the command of Rear-Admiral Cervera, has just performed the greatest deed of heroism that is perhaps recorded in the annals of the navy in the present century, fighting American forces three times as large. It succumbed gloriously, just when we considered it safe from the peril threatening it within the harbor of Santiago de Cuba. It is a hard blow, but it would be unworthy of Spanish hearts to despair.[82]

Following the crushing defeat of the Spanish navy off Santiago, action reverted to land. Shafter's divisions rested in the trenches outside the port town, awaiting the signal to close in on the enemy. Diplomatic moves, however, provided a solution that ended the bloodshed.

7 America's Increased Role in World Affairs

American arms had placed the nation in a position to dictate a favorable peace treaty. Like winners of all past conflicts, once the war ended, the nation's people eagerly awaited the fruits of victory, which in this case meant land. Citizens heralded the outcome and politicians proclaimed a new era for the United States. What they failed to understand was that the triumph, while invigorating, would usher in a new set of problems for the newcomer in terms of world politics.

SIEGE OF SANTIAGO

The most immediate concern now facing American military commanders was to end the war in Cuba before yellow fever and dysentery decimated the ranks. Once Santiago was taken, the United States could begin removing its soldiers before they succumbed to disease, but the longer they remained in front of the city, the more yellow fever would turn into a Spanish ally. Richard Harding Davis admitted as much when he wrote to his editor that he sensed a disaster approaching, and the army's surgeon general informed Shafter that "disease had driven its fangs into our men."[83]

With the advent of the wet season upon them, yellow fever and dysentery assumed larger roles in the lives of the soldiers. On July 26 alone, 639 new cases of yellow fever were diagnosed among the troops, and another 822 sought treatment the next day. Many never made it home alive. Private Charles Johnson Post recalled that "Each morning, we would hear bugles blowing taps very shortly after reveille [bugle sounding the morning wake-up call]. First, from off in the hills back of the trench line, a volley—the burial detail. Then the bugle. Taps, those slow, steady, and plaintive notes that mark the end of a day or the end of a soldier's life."[84]

Many of Shafter's subordinate officers, including Theodore Roosevelt, signed a document pleading for quick action. Called the "round-robin" letter because it was signed by every senior officer, the letter stated that "This army must be moved at once, or perish. As the army can be safely moved now, the persons responsible for preventing such a move will be responsible for the unnecessary loss of many thousands of lives."[85]

It was up to Shafter to decide when to begin the final assault on Santiago, but the officer was out of touch with the front lines. The overweight Shafter labored under the oppressive heat just to move around, so he remained in his tent for much of the campaign. When he left it to attend meetings with top officers, other soldiers had to carry him or lift him onto his horse. As a result he learned details about the fighting only from dispatches, casualty lists, and reports rather than firsthand observation.

This had drawbacks. For instance, Shafter worried about supplies not being more speedily whisked off the beaches, and he viewed with alarm the growing lists of American dead and wounded. On top of that came reports of a Spanish relief expedition from Manzanillo, Cuba, heading for Santiago. This caused him to question his

General William Shafter's hefty size hindered his ability to command his troops from the front lines.

top commanders about whether they should pull back from Santiago.

What he could not see was the enemy's sorry state of affairs, and that either a push by American soldiers or a firm demand of surrender could cause Spanish opposition to collapse. Continuous attacks by Cuban rebels were inflicting grave losses on Col. Federico Escario's relief force as it headed toward Santiago, and disease further cut into his numbers. Nonetheless, the relief column was within twenty miles of Santiago by July 2, and its arrival in the city was certain to stiffen Spanish resolve to continue the fight.

When three of the four senior officers urged Shafter not to pull back, the general agreed. However, instead of instantly attacking the city, before Escario arrived, Shafter wasted time bringing up more men and supplies and in considering the wording of a surrender demand. While Shafter lingered over these issues, Escario marched into Santiago and added his soldiers to the weary defenders.

Theodore Roosevelt and other officers were incensed at Shafter's tardiness. Roosevelt wrote that "Not since the campaign of [Roman commander] Crassus against the Parthians has there been so criminally incompetent a General as Shafter."[86] Shafter had the opportunity to swiftly finish the business but frittered it away in deliberations.

Shafter finally acted on July 3 by sending a surrender demand to Gen. Jose Toral. "Sir," the message stated, "I shall be obliged, unless you surrender, to shell Santiago de Cuba. Please inform the citizens of foreign countries and all women and children that they should leave the city before 10 o'clock tomorrow morning."[87] Not unexpectedly, Toral quickly rebuffed the offer.

SURRENDER AT SANTIAGO

Fortunately for historians, numerous newspaper correspondents covered the action in Cuba. One, Howbert Billman of the Chicago Record, *wrote down his observations of the surrender ceremony in an excerpt taken from Charles H. Brown's* The Correspondents' War:

"The cavalry was drawn up in line extending to the left of the road, General Shafter and the escorting generals taking position at the right. Their horses were hardly brought to a stand before General Toral appeared at the head of a Spanish column on the road. The Spanish commander and his escort reined their horses opposite General Shafter, and a battalion of Spanish infantry, with buglers at their head, marched before him and down the line of American cavalrymen at quickstep to the music of the Spanish bugle salute. When at the end of the line, they countermarched and our buglers chimed in with their salute. It was an odd medley of blaring notes, but extremely thrilling, that lasted until the Spanish were formed in line facing the cavalry. General Shafter rode forward a few paces and was met by General Toral. A few words of greeting, with the help of an interpreter, and the aide holding the latter's sword was summoned to restore it to its owner. The bugle salutes were repeated and the Spanish column marched back to the city, General Toral and his staff following."

When foreign dignitaries asked for more time to evacuate the twenty thousand women and children, Shafter agreed to postpone the shelling until July 5. On July 6, Shafter wrote Toral with another request to surrender. He threatened to move the U.S. fleet close to shore where it could leisurely bombard the city without fear of opposition. Shafter added that nothing could alter the fact that Spain would have to surrender, so why face further losses? He ended by giving Toral three more days to consider.

Shelling of Santiago began on July 10 after Shafter received no reply from Toral. The Americans had learned from evacuated civilians that the Spanish were suffering severe shortages in everything from food to ammunition, and that many soldiers were prepared to surrender. After two days, with no desire to add useless bloodshed to a hopeless cause, Toral sent word that he would like to discuss terms.

SURRENDER ENDS THE CONFLICT

Negotiations began on July 13 underneath a huge ceiba tree located in a valley between the Spanish and American lines. British vice-consul Robert Mason accompanied Toral as an interpreter, while Shafter led a delegation consisting of Gen. Nelson A. Miles (who would invade Puerto Rico on July 25), Wheeler, and an interpreter.

Negotiations proceeded at a friendly, leisurely pace. Observers commented on how affably the two sides appeared to treat each other and noticed the frequent smiles and instances of laughter. Over four days the opposing commanders hashed out an agreement, which was formally signed on July 17. Toral surrendered not only his 11,500 men in Santiago but the 12,000 soldiers fighting elsewhere on the island. A delighted Shafter wrote, "I was simply thunderstruck that, of their own free will, they should give me 12,000 men that were absolutely beyond my reach."[88] Opposition had ended and the Spanish-American War, at least in Cuba, was over. All that remained was for the respective governments to finalize the peace treaty.

American soldiers and correspondents were stunned by what they saw as they approached Santiago. According to correspondent James Archibald, animal carcasses littered the roads leading to the city. Vultures had dug open the shallow graves housing hastily buried Spanish soldiers and a sickening odor enveloped the entire area. But what most shocked the men was seeing what they would have faced in assaulting Santiago. Archibald wrote:

> The first barricade we encountered was the cleverly conceived barbed wire entanglement that did not close the road

General Toral meets with General Shafter on July 13, 1898, to negotiate the surrender of Santiago.

but compelled one entering to zigzag back and forth so that entrance under fire would have been next to impossible. Then came barricades of sand-filled barrels covering trenches. Side streets were blocked with paving stones, leaving loopholes [openings for Spanish riflemen to shoot through]. The thick-walled houses were also loopholed and would have made excellent fortifications. To have attempted to have taken the city by infantry assault would have meant the loss of thousands of our men.[89]

PEACE WITH SPAIN

With the fighting in Cuba at an end, the Spanish and U.S. governments moved to sign a peace document. Queen María Cristina sent a letter to McKinley in late July asking what his conditions for ending the war might be. She was prepared to hand Cuba to the United States, but the queen hoped to retain Puerto Rico, Guam, and the Philippines. McKinley replied that the Spanish must leave Cuba, grant Cubans their independence, and cede Guam and Puerto Rico to the United States. He also stated that the fate of the Philippines would be determined at a later date.

McKinley postponed his decision regarding the Philippines because the issue tormented him. He at first wanted to grant the Filipinos their independence, just as he demanded for Cuba, but he received intense pressure from political, military, and business interests to retain the islands. Many people in the United States, delighted with the nation's successful showing in the war,

favored keeping Cuba and the Philippines, and most major newspapers urged McKinley to annex the Philippines and place a major naval base in the islands.

A vocal minority spoke out against land acquisitions, however, claiming that such greedy measures defeated the spirit of equality and freedom upon which the nation had been built. Prominent politician and reformer Carl Schurz warned that

> The character and future of the Republic and the welfare of its people now living and yet to be born are in unprecedented jeopardy. The Filipinos fought against Spain for their freedom and independence, and unless they abandon their recently proclaimed purpose for their freedom and independence, they will fight against us.[90]

The president consulted with both Republicans and Democrats, but still could not resolve the issue. "I walked the floor of the White House night after night until midnight," he later said, "and I am not ashamed to tell you that I went down on my knees and prayed Almighty God for light and guidance more than one night."[91]

Finally, the solution materialized. McKinley concluded that it would be dishonorable to simply hand the Philippines back to Spain after American soldiers had sacrificed their lives. He could not allow any other nation to move into the power vacuum created by Spain's removal from the Philippines, because that would threaten growing American interest in the Pacific. He arrogantly dismissed the notion that the Filipinos could govern themselves because "they were unfit for self-government—and they would soon

Rather than granting the Filipinos independence, President McKinley claimed the Philippines for the United States.

have anarchy and misrule over there worse than Spain's was." By this process of elimination, McKinley concluded that

> there was nothing left for us to do but to take them all, and to educate the Filipinos, and uplift and civilize and Christianize them, and by God's grace do the very best we could by them, as our fellow-men for whom Christ also died. And then I went to bed, and went to sleep and slept soundly, and the next morning I sent for the chief engineer of the War Department (our mapmaker), and I told him to put the Philippines on the map of the United States, and there

they are, and there they will stay while I am President![92]

Negotiations eventually produced the December 10, 1898, Treaty of Paris. Cuba received its independence from Spain, although for a time the United States stepped into the role formerly held by Spain and exercised considerable power in the Caribbean island. Spain agreed to hand Puerto Rico and Guam to the United States, and the United States purchased the Philippines for $20 million.

The United States remained in Cuba for the next four years, gradually introducing reforms, more food and clothing, and improved education, farming practices, and sanitation. In May 1902 the United States formally recognized Cuban independence, but forced the Cubans to place in their new constitution the Platt Amendment to safeguard American interests on the island. The amendment stipulated that the United States had the right to intervene in Cuban affairs to protect life and maintain order, that Cuba could not agree to a treaty with any other nation unless the United States first approved it, and that the American navy could retain a naval base at Guantanamo Bay. In effect, the Cubans enjoyed only the appearance of freedom. With the Platt Amendment, the United States maintained a firm grip on Cuban affairs.

FIGHTING THE FILIPINOS

McKinley's decision to annex the Philippines had unexpected results. Aguinaldo, offended by Dewey's refusal to include

Filipinos in the peace negotiations and angered that Spanish rule appeared to be replaced with American dominance, in January 1899 proclaimed the Philippines an independent republic and started a protracted war for liberation.

Dewey asked for guidance from Washington about how to deal with the uprising. Could he use force? Should he resort only to negotiations with Aguinaldo? McKinley replied that Dewey and his commanders could "Use whatever means in your judgment are necessary to this end."[93]

Dewey wasted little time organizing his response. On February 4, 1899, near Manila, Dewey's ships fired into a concentration of rebel troops while American gunboats attacked along the Pasig River. The next day Army forces assaulted Aguinaldo's men posted in trenches outside Manila and forced them to fall back. A lengthy war between the Americans and the Filipinos had begun that would produce more violence and bloodshed than the entire Spanish-American War.

In November 1899, Maj. Gen. Elwell S. Otis arrived to replace General Merritt. Elwell organized a successful three-prong offensive against Aguinaldo that forced the rebel leader to flee into the mountains. At the same time Otis sent a force into Cavite Province to crush rebel units in that area.

To win the loyalty of Filipino civilians, McKinley ordered Otis to implement re-

The U.S. Army and Filipino rebels clash near Manila on February 5, 1899.

General Emilio Aguinaldo and his army during the insurrection against the United States in 1901.

forms. The U.S. Army built roads and bridges, installed telegraph lines, introduced health programs to eradicate cholera and smallpox, and improved the education system. The programs worked so well that Otis felt Aguinaldo's influence had been curtailed.

Otis erred in thinking that way, for the Filipino leader switched tactics. Instead of facing the U.S. Army in large clashes, he concentrated on smaller hit-and-run skirmishes. His men attacked, then suddenly melted into the jungle. They destroyed American lines of communication, impeded railway shipments of supplies, and ambushed American soldiers. Aguinaldo hoped this protracted fighting would undermine the willpower of the American public and lead to a withdrawal of U.S. troops.

Americans and Filipino rebels engaged in some of the most brutal forms of warfare. Prisoners were tortured to death or buried alive, and American soldiers, unsure about who was friend or foe, fired at Filipino civilians.

With the situation fast moving to the crisis level, McKinley sent Gen. Arthur MacArthur to succeed Otis. MacArthur, one of the Army's rising stars and father of future World War II great Douglas MacArthur, enacted harsher reprisals against the rebels while increasing the amount of assistance given to Filipino civilians. He issued orders to treat Aguinaldo's men without mercy because they would not follow the code of warfare, and gave his commanders authority to enact severe measures against towns suspected of aiding the rebels.

On March 23, 1901, MacArthur gained a huge victory in Palanan in northeast Luzon when a small unit of soldiers assisted by friendly Filipinos rushed Aguinaldo's hiding place and captured the rebel leader. This dramatic incident demoralized Aguinaldo's

ACTION IN PUERTO RICO

A final campaign ended the Caribbean fighting. One day after Toral's surrender, the U.S. War Department ordered General Miles to lead an invasion of Puerto Rico. The government wanted Puerto Rico as a coaling station and as a naval base to protect any future canal in Central America. He departed on July 21 for the four-day sea transit to the island and landed near Ponce on the island's south coast on July 25. A brief bombardment caused the small Spanish garrison in the area to pull back, allowing Miles to safely land his fifteen thousand soldiers.

Miles put into action a four-part plan to eliminate the Spanish on Puerto Rico. He sent the main thrust along the island's principal road, which connected Ponce with San Juan. Miles believed that this route, which wound through mountains, would be heavily defended by the Spanish and require the greatest effort. While this force battled north toward San Juan, a second contingent landed at Arroyo, forty-five miles east of Ponce, and moved out to cut off a retreat route for the Spanish facing Miles along the road. He sent a third unit to attack the western seaport of Mayagüez, and a fourth to assault Arecibo, thirty-five miles west of San Juan.

All four groups advanced against light opposition. The Spanish on Puerto Rico were not about to die in a useless cause, for they had already received the news of Cervera's defeat off Santiago and Toral's surrender of the town. The Americans fought six minor engagements and suffered forty-one casualties before learning in August that a peace agreement had been finalized with the Spanish government. Hostilities ceased on the island, which passed from Spanish control into the hands of the United States.

men, especially when Aguinaldo was taken under guard to Manila for incarceration.

Sadly, this did not end the bloodshed. On September 28, 1901, hundreds of Filipinos armed with huge knives called machetes swarmed an army campsite at Balangiga on the island of Samar and hacked to death forty-eight Americans.

When army officials learned that the rebels had mutilated the bodies, they sought vengeance. Brigadier General Jacob Smith bluntly ordered his soldiers, "I wish you to kill and burn; the more you kill and burn the better it will please me. I want all persons killed who are capable of bearing arms in actual hostilities against the United States."[94] When an officer asked what age Smith considered capable of bearing arms, the general said anyone age ten and over.

The tactics, however stringent, produced results. By July 4, 1902, President Theodore Roosevelt, who had risen to office following the assassination of McKinley, declared the fighting in the Philippines over. Four years of killing in two oceans had finally come to an end.

NEW RESPONSIBILITIES

The Spanish-American War prompted a decade of land acquisitions by the United States. After annexing Hawaii in August 1898, the nation added Guam, Puerto Rico, and the Philippines, and exerted considerable control in Cuba. The United States could now count itself among the exclusive community of world powers, along with England, France, Germany, Russia, Austria-Hungary, and Italy, and the nation's military commanded more respect from European rivals.

The benefits had not come cheaply. The American military suffered 5,400 deaths in Cuba (only 379 from battle, the rest from disease and accidents) and another 4,200 in the Philippines. More than 20,000 Filipino soldiers died, and ferocious combat, harsh reprisals, and disease cost up to 200,000 civilian deaths.

An elevated status throughout the world also brought its own set of responsibilities and problems. For the first time in the nation's history the United States was now involved in the affairs of other countries, partly as colonial overseer and partly as a member of the exclusive community of world powers. In this role the nation would face crises that required commitments of time, money, and military.

For instance, to protect its newfound interests in Puerto Rico and Cuba, the United States had to become more visible in Caribbean affairs. Prior to the Spanish-American War the nation had concentrated on issues and problems at home—settling the West, expanding an economy, forging lucrative business enterprises, and rebuilding the country after the Civil War. After the Spanish-American War, the country's energies turned more toward the world stage. Not only was the United States dragged into World War I (1917–1918, the first time American soldiers fought on European battlefields), it was engaged in brutal conflicts in Korea and Vietnam, and later sent troops to different "hotspots" to secure American interests at home and abroad.

This increased role in world affairs delighted expansionists and dismayed those who opposed colonial possessions. Theodore Roosevelt never ceased touting the benefits of being a world power and repeating that the country had a duty to expand, build a

Throughout his presidency, Roosevelt continued to favor the expansion of American foreign power.

stronger military, and inform European powers that a new nation had risen to their ranks. He mentioned in an 1898 speech, "There comes a time in the life of a nation, as in the life of an individual, when it must face great responsibilities. We have now reached that time. We cannot avoid facing the fact that we occupy a new place among the people of the world, and have entered upon a new career."[95]

Opponents took a different view. Moorfield Storey, a Boston reformer who opposed American expansionism, warned that the nation was headed toward unforeseen perils with its more active role in world affairs and would be dragged into unwanted complications in possessions thousands of miles away. He said that should the United States "reach out for fresh territory, to our present difficulties would be added an agitation for the annexation of new regions which, unfit to govern themselves, would govern us. God grant that such calamities are not in store for us."[96]

Author Mark Twain stated the case against expansion even more bluntly. He wrote that the U.S. flag should be modified so that "the white stripes [are] painted black and the stars replaced by the skull and cross bones."[97]

WELCOME HOME?

Once back in the United States, the soldiers returned to the customs of American society, which meant that not every man who fought at San Juan Hill, El Caney, or with Roosevelt at Kettle Hill received equal treatment. As Page Smith related in *The Rise of Industrial America*, one African American soldier wrote of the men from the Ninth and Tenth Cavalry that while they fought and bled for the same flag as their white brethren, "these black boys, heroes of our country, were not allowed to stand at the counters of the restaurants and eat a sandwich and drink a cup of coffee, while the white soldiers were welcomed and invited to sit down at the tables and eat free of cost. There are but few places in this country, if any, where the hatred of the Negro is not."

Roosevelt did his best to make black troops feel appreciated upon their return. The members of the Rough Riders presented Roosevelt a beautiful bronze statue of a horseman riding a bucking bronco, done by Frederic Remington, to show their appreciation of what Roosevelt had done for them in Cuba. When Roosevelt offered words of thanks, he noticed a group of black troopers watching from a distance, turned to them, and praised them for their courageous showing under fire. According to Page Smith he added, "Outside of my own family, I shall never show as strong ties as I do toward you." He then walked up and shook each man's hand. The nation may not have welcomed the black soldiers with open arms, but Roosevelt wanted to show, from one soldier to another, what he thought of their contributions.

Admiral Dewey and President McKinley (in carriage) are honored by patriotic Americans during a victory parade after the Spanish-American War.

THE LEGACY OF THE WAR

On the home front, the war helped reunite a country that had been bitterly divided since the Civil War forty years earlier. Although the nation had been gradually healing its wounds in the intervening years, it was not until the country rallied behind its soldiers in the Spanish-American War that the final traces of disunity were removed. Young men from all sections of the nation rushed to recruiting centers and headed to Cuba or the Philippines on troop transports—all as part of the same army. Families from Northern and Southern states cheered the same mili-

tary, rejoiced over common victories, and shed tears for soldiers slain fighting side by side rather than against each other. Old wounds had been relegated to the past and the nation looked ahead as one people.

Theodore Roosevelt's career received an enormous boost, not that the enthusiastic leader needed much help. He and the Rough Riders became national heroes, and he deftly parlayed this military fame into the governorship of New York. He advanced from that post to become McKinley's vice president in 1901, then assumed the powers of chief executive in the wake of McKinley's assassination that same year.

The nation rarely saw anything like Roosevelt's eight years as president. The energetic politician introduced reform in soil conservation, butted heads with business titans, gave renewed hope to labor unions and advocates of safer workplaces, and pushed for laws guaranteeing safer products from the food and drug industries. Theodore Roosevelt altered the nation's landscape during his tenure as chief executive, and the seeds for his presidency were sewn in the fields and slopes of Cuba.

The most far-reaching effect of the Spanish-American War did not completely unfold until December 1941. With vested interests in the Pacific, the United States had to create a navy to protect those possessions from aggressor nations, and that placed the country on a path that inevitably led to conflict. Japan, seeking to rise in status in much the same way the United States had with the Spanish-American War, had already begun making noises in the Far East, and one day would cast covetous eyes toward the Philippines and Guam, and angry eyes at a little-known American naval base in Pearl Harbor, Hawaii.

Japan, still busy in 1902 building a foundation for military dominance on the Asian mainland, would shortly rise to challenge the United States for supremacy in the Pacific. Just as the seeds for Theodore Roosevelt's presidency were sewn in this conflict, so too were the roots of World War II nurtured by the fighting between Spain and the United States.

Notes

Introduction: Little War, Big Effects

1. Quoted in Samuel Eliot Morison and Henry Steele Commager, *The Growth of the American Republic*. New York: Oxford University Press, 1962, p. 427.

Chapter 1: A Desire to Acquire Power and Wealth

2. Quoted in Morison and Commager, *The Growth of the American Republic*, p. 414.

3. Quoted in Morison and Commager, *The Growth of the American Republic*, p. 415.

4. Quoted in G. J. A. O'Toole, *The Spanish War*. New York: W. W. Norton, 1984, p. 36.

5. Quoted in O'Toole, *The Spanish War*, p. 56.

6. Quoted in Donald M. Goldstein, Katherine V. Dillon, J. Michael Wenger, and Robert J. Cressman, *The Spanish-American War: The Story and Photographs*. Washington, DC: Brassey's, 1998, pp. 9–10.

7. Quoted in O'Toole, *The Spanish War*, p. 25.

Chapter 2: "A Terrible Mass of Fire and Explosion"

8. Quoted in Morison and Commager, *The Growth of the American Republic*, p. 420.

9. Quoted in Page Smith, *The Rise of Industrial America*. New York: McGraw-Hill, 1984, p. 864.

10. Quoted in Smith, *The Rise of Industrial America*, p. 865.

11. Quoted in Goldstein, Dillon, Wenger, and Cressman, *The Spanish-American War*, p. 26.

12. Quoted in Morison and Commager, *The Growth of the American Republic*, p. 416.

13. Quoted in David F. Trask, *The War with Spain in 1898*. Lincoln: University of Nebraska Press, 1981, p. 28.

14. Quoted in Allan Keller, *The Spanish-American War: A Compact History*. New York: Hawthorn Books, 1969, p. 35.

15. Quoted in O'Toole, *The Spanish War*, p. 29.

16. Quoted in O'Toole, *The Spanish War*, pp. 29–30.

17. Quoted in Charles H. Brown, *The Correspondents' War: Journalists in the Spanish-American War*. New York: Charles Scribner's Sons, 1967, p. 116.

18. Quoted in O'Toole, *The Spanish War*, p. 31.

19. Quoted in Brown, *The Correspondents' War*, pp. 117–18.

20. Quoted in Brown, *The Correspondents' War*, p. 124.

21. Quoted in Goldstein, Dillon, Wenger, and Cressman, *The Spanish-American War*, p. 15.

22. Quoted in Kenneth J. Hagan, *This People's Navy: The Making of American Sea Power*. New York: Free Press, 1991, p. 214.

23. Quoted in O'Toole, *The Spanish War*, p. 125.

24. Quoted in Stephen Howarth, *To Shining Sea: A History of the United States Navy, 1775–1991*. New York: Random House, 1991, p. 249.

25. Quoted in Trask, *The War with Spain in 1898*, p. 35.

Chapter 3: "There Are Limits to Everything"

26. Quoted in Hagan, *This People's Navy*, p. 214.

27. Quoted in H. W. Brands, *T. R.: The Last Romantic*. New York: BasicBooks, 1997, p. 326.

28. Quoted in Brands, *T. R.: The Last Romantic*, p. 327.

29. Quoted in Trask, *The War with Spain in 1898*, p. 45.

30. Quoted in Howarth, *To Shining Sea*, p. 250.

31. Trask, *The War with Spain in 1898*, p. 59.

32. Quoted in O'Toole, *The Spanish War*, p. 225.

33. Quoted in Smith, *The Rise of Industrial America*, p. 875.

34. Quoted in O'Toole, *The Spanish War*, p. 195.

35. Quoted in Trask, *The War with Spain in 1898*, pp. 63–64.

36. Quoted in Howarth, *To Shining Sea*, pp. 252–53.

Chapter 4: A Lopsided Victory

37. George Dewey, *Autobiography of George Dewey*. Annapolis: Naval Institute Press, 1987, p. 73.

38. Quoted in Laurin Hall Healy and Luis Kutner, *The Admiral*. Chicago: Ziff-Davis, 1944, pp. 127–28.

39. Theodore Roosevelt, *Theodore Roosevelt: An Autobiography*. New York: Macmillan, 1915, p. 86.

40. Quoted in Healy and Kutner, *The Admiral*, p. 171n.

41. Quoted in O'Toole, *The Spanish War*, p. 174.

42. Quoted in Ronald Spector, *Admiral of the New Empire*. Baton Rouge: Louisiana State University Press, 1974, p. 51.

43. Quoted in Mark Sullivan, *Our Times, Volume I*. New York: Scribner's, 1927, p. 315.

44. Quoted in Healy and Kutner, *The Admiral*, pp. 174–75.

45. Quoted in Brown, *The Correspondents' War*, p. 191.

46. Joseph L. Stickney, "With Dewey at Manila," *Harper's Magazine*, February 1899, p. 479.

47. Dewey, *Autobiography of George Dewey*, p. 191.

48. Quoted in Brown, *The Correspondents' War*, p. 193.

49. Stickney, "With Dewey at Manila," pp. 476–77.

50. Quoted in Howarth, *To Shining Sea*, p. 257.

51. Quoted in Brown, *The Correspondents' War*, p. 183.

52. Quoted in Allan R. Millett and Peter Maslowski, *For the Common Defense: A Military History of the United States of America*. New York: Free Press, 1984, p. 275.

Chapter 5: "The Great Day"

53. Quoted in Brown, *The Correspondents' War*, p. 281.

54. Quoted in O'Toole, *The Spanish War*, p. 248.

55. Quoted in Goldstein, Dillon, Wenger, and Cressman, *The Spanish-American War*, p. 84.

56. Quoted in Edmund Morris, *The Rise of Theodore Roosevelt*. New York: Ballantine Books, 1979, p. 637.

57. Quoted in Morris, *The Rise of Theodore Roosevelt*, p. 639.

58. Quoted in Trask, *The War with Spain in 1898*, p. 228.

59. Quoted in Morris, *The Rise of Theodore Roosevelt*, p. 636.

60. Quoted in Morris, *The Rise of Theodore Roosevelt*, p. 648.

61. Quoted in O'Toole, *The Spanish War*, p. 274.

62. Quoted in Morris, *The Rise of Theodore Roosevelt*, p. 650.

63. Quoted in O'Toole, *The Spanish War*, p. 321.

64. Theodore Roosevelt, *The Rough Riders*. New York: New American Library, 1961, pp. 79–80.

65. Quoted in Roosevelt, *The Rough Riders*, p. 83.

66. Quoted in Morris, *The Rise of Theodore Roosevelt*, p. 654.

67. Roosevelt, *The Rough Riders*, p. 87.

68. Quoted in Smith, *The Rise of Industrial America*, p. 876.

69. Quoted in Bernard C. Nalty, *Strength for the Fight: A History of Black Americans in the Military*. New York: Free Press, 1986, p. 71.

70. Roosevelt, *The Rough Riders*, p. 92.

Chapter 6: Spain's Defeat

71. Quoted in Goldstein, Dillon, Wenger, and Cressman, *The Spanish-American War*, p. 62.

72. Quoted in Brown, *The Correspondents' War*, p. 292.

73. Quoted in O'Toole, *The Spanish War*, p. 236.

74. Quoted in Brown, *The Correspondents' War*, p. 294.

75. Quoted in Goldstein, Dillon, Wenger, and Cressman, *The Spanish-American War*, p. 121.

76. Quoted in Goldstein, Dillon, Wenger, and Cressman, *The Spanish-American War*, p. 124.

77. Quoted in O'Toole, *The Spanish War*, p. 331.

78. Quoted in O'Toole, *The Spanish War*, p. 335.

79. Quoted in Goldstein, Dillon, Wenger, and Cressman, *The Spanish-American War*, p. 125.

80. Quoted in Goldstein, Dillon, Wenger, and Cressman, *The Spanish-American War*, p. 129.

81. Quoted in Howarth, *To Shining Sea*, p. 269.

82. Quoted in O'Toole, *The Spanish War*, p. 341.

Chapter 7: America's Increased Role in World Affairs

83. Quoted in Keller, *The Spanish-American War*, p. 173.

84. Quoted in O'Toole, *The Spanish War*, p. 358.

85. Quoted in Morris, *The Rise of Theodore Roosevelt*, p. 660.

86. Quoted in O'Toole, *The Spanish War*, p. 346.

87. Quoted in Keller, *The Spanish-American War*, p. 177.

88. Quoted in Brown, *The Correspondents' War*, p. 399.

89. Quoted in Brown, *The Correspondents' War*, p. 402.

90. Quoted in Brands, *T. R.: The Last Romantic*, p. 384.

91. Quoted in O'Toole, *The Spanish War*, p. 386.

92. Quoted in O'Toole, *The Spanish War*, p. 386.

93. Quoted in Millett and Maslowski, *For the Common Defense*, p. 289.

94. Quoted in Millett and Maslowski, *For the Common Defense*, p. 295.

95. Quoted in Brands, *T. R.: The Last Romantic*, p. 366.

96. Quoted in Trask, *The War with Spain in 1898*, pp. 53–54.

97. Quoted in Morison and Commager, *The Growth of the American Republic*, p. 430.

For Further Reading

Robert Conroy, *The Battle of Manila Bay*. New York: Macmillan, 1968. Conroy has written a sound account of the fighting in the Philippines for junior high school students. This aspect of the war frequently receives inadequate treatment, but Conroy corrects that with this book.

Jean Fritz, *Bully for You, Teddy Roosevelt!* New York: G. P. Putnam's Sons, 1991. An outstanding biography of Theodore Roosevelt for junior high school students. Written in an engaging style, the book is a triumph of writing and information.

John A. Garraty, *Theodore Roosevelt: The Strenuous Life*. New York: Harper & Row, 1967. Part of the illustrious *American Heritage* Junior Library series and written by a well-known historian, this book provides a complete look at Roosevelt. Junior high school students will find this very helpful.

Kerry A. Graves, *The Spanish-American War*. Mankato, MN: Capstone Press, 2000. A brief history of the war that provides much useful information.

Joy Hakim, *An Age of Extremes*. New York: Oxford University Press, 1994. The book, a volume in Hakim's heralded history of the United States for young readers, contains a fine overview of the Spanish-American War.

George P. Hunt, *The Story of the U.S. Marines*. New York: Random House, 1951. This history of the Marine Corps, written for grades 5–8, includes a brief account of the assault at Guantanamo Bay.

Zachary Kent, *The Story of the Sinking of the Battleship Maine*. Chicago: Childrens Press, 1988. This book, which focuses on the origins of the fighting in Cuba, serves as a helpful complement to Conroy's book on the fighting in the Philippines.

J. Phillip Langellier, *Uncle Sam's Little Wars*. New York: Greenhill Books, 1999. A very fine examination of the fighting in Cuba and the Philippines.

Red Reeder, *The Story of the Spanish-American War*. New York: Duell, Sloan, and Pearce, 1966. Reeder uses his military background to good purpose with a helpful history of the war with Spain. Students in grades 6–10 will find this helpful.

Dale L. Walker, *The Boys of '98: Theodore Roosevelt and the Rough Riders*. New York: Forge Publishing, 1998. Walker's book depicts Theodore Roosevelt and his famed unit. The author captures the excitement of the times and explains why the Rough Riders gained fame after the war.

John Walsh, *The Sinking of the USS Maine, February 15, 1898*. New York: Franklin Watts, 1969. This is a good, brief account of the sinking that started the war, written for grades 5–8.

Irving Werstein, *Turning Point for America: The Story of the Spanish-American War*. New York: Julian Messner, 1964. A good, brief account of the war for young readers.

Works Consulted

H. W. Brands, *T. R.: The Last Romantic.* New York: BasicBooks, 1997. Brands has written one of the liveliest available biographies of Roosevelt. The material covering Roosevelt's actions in Cuba and how those actions elevated him to the presidency is especially good.

Charles H. Brown, *The Correspondents' War: Journalists in the Spanish-American War.* New York: Charles Scribner's Sons, 1967. Brown examines the role of reporters and newspaper publishers in the war. His lively writing is assisted by many quotes taken from the writing of those reporters.

Gerald A. Danzer, J. Jorge Klor de Alva, Louis E. Wilson, and Nancy Woloch, *The Americans.* Evanston, Illinois: McDougal Littel, 1999. This survey of the United States from the Civil War to modern times offers an excellent chapter on the Spanish-American War.

George Dewey, *Autobiography of George Dewey.* Annapolis: Naval Institute Press, 1987. Written fifteen years after the end of the war, this is a valuable account of the fighting in the Philippines by the commander of the American Asiatic Squadron.

Donald M. Goldstein, Katherine V. Dillon, J. Michael Wenger, and Robert J. Cressman, *The Spanish-American War: The Story and Photographs.* Washington, DC: Brassey's, 1998. The authors assemble a superb summation of the war and it is especially powerful in describing the causes of the war and the action in and near Cuba. Numerous photographs supplement the text.

Kenneth J. Hagan, *This People's Navy: The Making of American Sea Power.* New York: Free Press, 1991. Hagan compiles a good basic history of the United States, which includes a chapter on the naval aspects of the Spanish-American War.

Laurin Hall Healy and Luis Kutner, *The Admiral.* Chicago: Ziff-Davis, 1944. An excellent biography of Admiral Dewey that is easy to read and filled with useful material.

Stephen Howarth, *To Shining Sea: A History of the United States Navy, 1775–1991.* New York: Random House, 1991. Noted naval historian Howarth provides an excellent summary of U.S. naval history, with an especially readable chapter on the Spanish-American War.

Allan Keller, *The Spanish-American War: A Compact History.* New York: Hawthorn Books, 1969. This informative book provides a general account of the war. Its lively style makes it fun to read.

Allan R. Millet, *Semper Fidelis: The History of the United States Marine Corps.* New York: Macmillan, 1980. A fine military historian, Millet covers the role of the U.S. Marines in Cuba during the war.

Allan R. Millett and Peter Maslowski, *For the Common Defense: A Military History of the United States of America.* New York: Free Press, 1984. Two eminent military historians compile a superb general history of U.S. military action through the years. Their chapter on the Spanish-American War, like the other chapters, resonates with clarity and organization.

Samuel Eliot Morison and Henry Steele Commager, *The Growth of the American Republic*. New York: Oxford University Press, 1962. Morison and Commager produced possibly the finest survey of American history with this book. It includes a superb chapter explaining the causes and effects of the Spanish-American War.

Edmund Morris, *The Rise of Theodore Roosevelt*. New York: Ballantine Books, 1979. This biography, one of the finest books ever written about Theodore Roosevelt, contains valuable material on the fighting in Cuba from Roosevelt's point of view. Morris has produced an outstanding piece of writing.

Bernard C. Nalty, *Strength for the Fight: A History of Black Americans in the Military*. New York: Free Press, 1986. This book superbly covers the experiences of African Americans in the military. Like every other chapter, the one dealing with the Spanish-American War provides abundant helpful information.

G. J. A. O'Toole, *The Spanish War*. New York: W. W. Norton, 1984. This comprehensive look at the Spanish-American War is clearly written. The author's use of quotations helps enliven the text. This is one of the best books on the topic.

Theodore Roosevelt, *The Rough Riders*. New York: New American Library, 1961. Written shortly after the war, Roosevelt's personal account focuses upon the contributions made by Roosevelt and the Rough Riders. Roosevelt delivers a fascinating glimpse of Americans at war.

Theodore Roosevelt, *Theodore Roosevelt: An Autobiography*. New York: Macmillan, 1915. A thorough exposition of his life, influences, and contributions, written by one of the most vibrant individuals to occupy the presidency.

Page Smith, *The Rise of Industrial America*. New York: McGraw-Hill, 1984. Smith produces a very readable history of the United States during the latter half of the nineteenth century. He includes numerous quotes throughout the manuscript.

Ronald Spector, *Admiral of the New Empire*. Baton Rouge: Louisiana State University Press, 1974. A biography written by a naval expert, the book focuses more on technical details rather than a personal biography of Admiral Dewey.

Joseph L. Stickney, "With Dewey at Manila," *Harper's Magazine*, February 1899. A valuable article written by a newspaper correspondent who stood next to Admiral Dewey on the flagship during the battle.

Mark Sullivan, *Our Times, Volume I*. New York: Scribner's, 1927. Sullivan wrote a six-volume history of the United States at the turn of the century. He fills the books with fascinating information and glimpses of life, culture, trends, and advances.

David F. Trask, *The War with Spain in 1898*. Lincoln: University of Nebraska Press, 1981. Trask's very thorough account of the war is, along with O'Toole's book, the best source of information available.

Index

prepares for war, 44–45
on Roosevelt's desire to
charge into battle,
43–44
Luzon, 93

MacArthur, Arthur, 93
MacArthur, Douglas, 93
Mahan, Alfred T., 15
Maine (U.S. battleship),
26–28, 30–34
manifest destiny, 15
Manila, 46, 49–51, 57–60, 92
Manila Bay, 49–51, 53, 59
Manila Punch, 58
Manzanillo, 87
Marblehead (U.S. cruiser),
61, 74
María Cristina (queen of
Spain), 37–38, 90
Maria Teresa (Spanish
flagship), 79, 80–81
marines. *See* United States,
Marine Corps
Marques del Duero (Spanish
gunboat), 50
Marshall, Edward, 66, 68
Martí, José, 18
Martinique, 75
Mason, Robert, 88
Mayagüez, 94
McCalla, Bowman H., 74
McCulloch (U.S. cutter), 48,
53
McKinley, William
appointments by
Dewey as Asiatic
Squadron
commander, 48
former Confederate
officers to high
posts, 44

asks Congress to
intervene in Cuba, 38
asks Spain to leave Cuba,
90
asks volunteers to join
National Guard, 39
assassination of, 11
becomes president of
United States, 22–23
de Lôme harshly
criticizes, 26
demands improvement
of conditions in Cuba,
24–25, 36–37
orders Dewey not to
contact Filipino rebel
forces, 59
orders *Maine* to Cuba, 27
orders Otis to implement
reforms in Philippines,
92–93
reaction to early news
reports about war in
Philippines, 57
receives Dewey's report
on war's outcome in
Philippines, 58
sends MacArthur to
replace Otis in
Philippines, 93
signs peace agreement
with Spain, 60
on starting war with
Spain, 34
McMillan, James L., 68
Merrimac (U.S. collier),
77–78
Merritt, Wesley, 59, 92
Mexico, 14
Mexico City, 14
Miles, Nelson A., 89, 94
Millett, Allan R., 62
Mississippi River, 47

Montojo y Pasaron, Don
Patricio, 50, 52, 57

Nanshan (U.S. collier), 48
Nashville (U.S. gunboat), 74
National Guard, 39
New Orleans, 47
New Spain, 14
New York City Police
Department, 23
New York Herald
(newspaper), 66
New York Journal
(newspaper)
de Lôme letter published
in, 26
Marshall writes about
fighting at Las
Guasimas in, 66, 68
newspaper war between
New York World and, 24
popularity of Davis's
articles in, 19
report about American
athletes scaring
Spanish in, 41
reports on *Maine*
explosion in, 32
on Weyler's rule in
Cuba, 21
New York State Assembly, 23
New York Tribune
(newspaper), 57
New York World
(newspaper), 24, 26, 53
Nicaragua, 16
Ninth Cavalry, 43, 70–72, 96
North Atlantic Squadron, 44

Olympia (U.S. flagship), 48,
51–56
O'Neill, William O.
"Bucky," 70

Picture Credits

Cover: Archive Photos

American Stock/Archive Photos, 71

Archive Photos, 35, 47, 63, 79

© Bettmann/Corbis, 12, 29, 93, 95

© Dr. Christian Brandstäter (d/b/a Austrian Archives)/Corbis, 38

© Corbis, 22, 23, 83

Collection of The New York Historical Society, 39

Hulton Getty/Archive Photos, 17, 18, 20, 42

Library of Congress, 19, 25, 28, 31, 32, 40, 44, 49, 53, 55, 67, 69, 72, 82, 89, 92, 97

National Archives, 27, 30, 36, 43, 56, 59, 64, 81, 87

North Wind Picture Archives, 45, 66, 70, 84

Martha Schierholz, 73, 76

U.S. Naval Historical Center, 33, 51, 58, 75, 77, 80, 91

About the Author

John F. Wukovits is a junior high school teacher and writer from Trenton, Michigan, who specializes in history and biography. Besides biographies of Anne Frank, Jim Carrey, Stephen King, and Martin Luther King Jr. for Lucent Books, he has written biographies of World War II commander Adm. Clifton Sprague, Barry Sanders, Tim Allen, Jack Nicklaus, Vince Lombardi, and Wyatt Earp. A graduate of the University of Notre Dame, Wukovits is the father of three daughters—Amy, Julie, and Karen.